COMPUTER BASICS

VOLUME 6

SOLID-STATE COMPUTER CIRCUITS

by
TECHNICAL EDUCATION AND
MANAGEMENT, INC.

HOWARD W. SAMS & CO., INC.
THE BOBBS-MERRILL CO., INC.
INDIANAPOLIS · KANSAS CITY · NEW YORK

Preface

Solid-state computers are rapidly superseding their vacuum-tube counterparts. The reasons are simple and compelling—semi-conductors are rugged and reliable, are ideal for modular or building-block design, have much greater operating speeds, result in smaller and lighter equipment, and reduce power consumption and heat generation. The trend is toward the application of still newer solid-state devices, including the tunnel diode, to which an entire chapter in this volume is devoted.

The purpose of this book is to provide a practical treatment of transistorized circuits in logic and arithmetic elements, as well as in magnetic-core devices which have largely taken over the memory function in computers. Emphasis is placed on basic theory and practice, supplemented where necessary by equations and design considerations. This approach is augmented by the inclusion of component values and semiconductor types in most of the illustrations.

Operational amplifiers, electronic multipliers, and other transistorized circuits are discussed in detail in the chapters on analog computers. Special attention is given to such digital-computer topics as transistor and tunnel-diode switching characteristics, transistor flip-flops, as well as AND, OR, and transistor-driven core logic. Circuits common to both analog and digital equipment, such as regulated power supplies and emitter followers are also described.

Packaging of solid-state circuitry has become increasingly important; thus, an entire chapter has been devoted to this subject. Printed, potted, and deposited-film methods are treated in depth, as are the principles of the universally-accepted modular-construction techniques.

Maintenance procedures and equipment, often ignored in books of this nature, are covered in the final chapter. An entire gamut of subjects, ranging from module testers and marginal testing procedures through modular repair techniques, are illustrated and discussed.

We wish to thank the many manufacturers who have so generously provided the latest information and data used in preparing this volume. Special thanks are extended to Robert L. Snyder—supervisor–instructor of the Computer Basics course conducted at U. S. Naval Electronics School, Service School Command, Great Lakes, Illinois—for his participation in preparing the manuscript.

Technical Education and
Management, Inc.

Table of Contents

CHAPTER 1

Computers and Building-Block Circuits

Any computer is composed of a few basic circuits, which perform a multitude of jobs. The operational amplifier is the heart of any electronic analog computer, which may use hundreds of these circuits. The average digital computer, on the other hand, will consist of thousands of combinations using five basic *logic* circuits as "building blocks" to make up the entire system. As shown in Fig. 1-1, most modern computers use transistorized circuits because of the savings in space and power which transistors provide.

This book will show how these transistorized circuits work. In addition, it will present the over-all characteristics of analog and digital computers, along with information on how these

(Courtesy Packard-Bell Electronics Corp.)
Fig. 1-1. Transistorized computer circuits.

circuits are connected so that they are able to perform computations and control functions. The main concentration, however, will be on circuits, since the other volumes in the *Computer Basics Series* contain detailed discussions of the other aspects of analog and digital computers.

WHAT ARE COMPUTERS?

Computers are devices which process input data that represents numerical quantities to provide output data which represents mathematical relationships between these input quantities. The most obvious application of computers is for con-

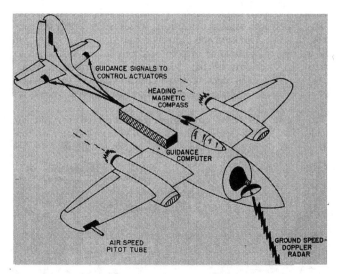

Fig. 1-2. Computer-guided aircraft.

verting numbers into sums, differences, products, and quotients at the output. In this sense, the adding machine or desk calculator is a computer. However, in a much broader sense, such computation is only one small part of the over-all process.

Suppose a computer is to guide an aircraft (which is not really a supposition, since such computers do exist). The inputs to this computer are electrical quantities representing the response of sensing elements to air speed, ground speed, and to the magnetic-compass indication of heading. The computer (Fig. 1-2) is "told" where the aircraft is to go by the insertion

8

of the latitude and longitude information pertaining to the desired destination. The output of this computer system will then regulate the movement of the control surfaces on the aircraft, causing it to fly toward and arrive at that destination.

The point is that computers are capable of performing control operations based on their computations. In a sense, the computer of a control system is similar to the human brain. In the human system, as shown in Fig. 1-3, the input data comes from sense elements such as the eyes, ears, nose, tongue, and skin sensors (nerves). Computations are performed by the brain, which is "told" what the desired result is to be. The brain then sends control signals to the muscles, which cause the whole body to carry out an operation leading to that result.

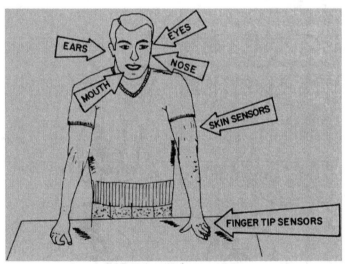

Fig. 1-3. Organic data-converters.

In the broader sense mentioned, computers (over-all control systems using computers) are devices capable of processing input data concerning their physical environment in order to provide output data (specifically related to the input data) which cause the desired modification of that physical environment.

At this point, computers and control systems may seem quite complex. However, it will be shown that the most complex operations can be accomplished by interconnected groups of simple circuits and components. In fact, once understood, the interconnections are relatively simple, also.

9

COMPUTER OPERATIONS

The most complex computer operations can be broken down into a series of simple steps, which are accomplished by use of circuits to be explained later. These steps (Fig. 1-4) are:

1. Data conversion to electrical quantities.
2. Addition.
3. Subtraction.
4. Multiplication.
5. Division.
6. Comparison.
7. Data transfer.
8. Data storage.
9. Operation sequencing and timing.
10. Yes-no decision making.
11. Data conversion to desired form.

Fig. 1-4. Operations performed by computers.

Data Conversion To Electrical Quantities

Data conversion to electrical quantities, as shown in Fig. 1-5, is the first operation performed by any electronic computer. Analog computers often must convert hydraulic, mechanical, or thermal quantities into electrical. For example, if an analog

10

computer is processing heat data, the measured temperature is converted into a voltage representing that temperature. This is often done by circuits having a resistance or voltage which varies with temperature. Any device which converts data from one form to another is called a *converter*.

Digital computers must use converters, also. An example is the machine which reads punched tape or punched cards. It converts the *position* of the holes in the material into electrical pulses having numerical values based on those positions. That is, the digit *2* represents *20* when it is in the *10's place (20)*.

THERMOCOUPLE

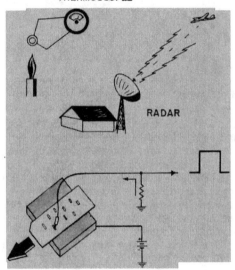

PUNCHED-CARD READER

Fig. 1-5. Converters which convert data into electrical form.

Computer control systems use many converters in order to express all system quantities in electrical form. In industrial systems, mechanical devices are actuated by units on a conveyer belt in order to give a switch closure and opening for the passage of each unit. This switch action, when connected to a voltage source, provides a voltage pulse each time a unit passes the "counting station." In aviation control systems, a radar set provides a pulse each time its beam passes an airborne aircraft. In the first system the switch, and in the second the radar, are counting stations. Of course the radar also provides data indi-

11

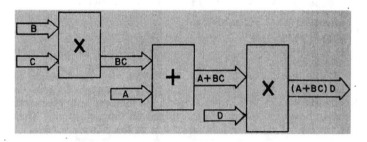

Fig. 1-6. Arithmetic operations performed by a computer.

cating distance and bearing of the aircraft. The important thing
to remember, however, is that both systems are data converters.

Arithmetic Operations

Computers use circuits that can add, subtract, multiply, and
divide (Fig. 1-6). A common circuit that can multiply a changing voltage by a constant number is an amplifier.

Analog computers operate on voltages whose *magnitude*
(value in volts) represent numbers, as shown in Fig. 1-7. Thus,
the quantity 5 might be represented by a 5-volt DC signal. This
number can be multiplied by a constant (13 for example) by
passing it through an amplifier (Fig. 1-8) with a gain of 13. If a
slowly varying voltage ("X") were applied to this amplifier,
the output would always be 13X. The result can be read on an
oscilloscope, in much the same way that values of a curve can
be read from graph paper.

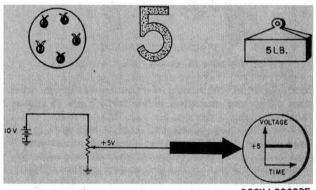

OSCILLOSCOPE

Fig. 1-7. Analog computers use voltage levels to represent numbers.

12

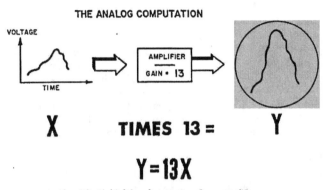

THE ANALOG COMPUTATION

$$Y=13X$$

Fig. 1-8. Multiplying by means of an amplifier.

In the digital computer the operations are called arithmetic, but are performed in a slightly different way. Basically, a digital computer can only add. If multiplication is desired, it is accomplished by repeated adding (Fig. 1-9). 3 times 5 actually means to add 3 five times or to add 5 three times. In other words, any two numbers can be multiplied by adding one of them to itself the number of times indicated by the other number.

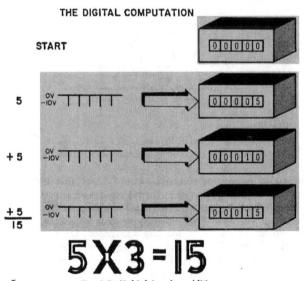

THE DIGITAL COMPUTATION

Fig. 1-9. Multiplying by addition.

The digital computer uses pulses to represent numbers. The number 5, as in Fig. 1-10 for example, could be represented by five pulses generated one after another. Numbers can be added by applying the pulses representing the one number to a pulse counter the number of times indicated by the other number. The resulting count will represent the product of the two numbers. Thus, if 5 is added three times, the product of 5 times 3 is obtained.

Pulses are also used in digital computers to represent numbers in ways other than merely supplying the same number of pulses as the number being represented. These other numbers (binary) are discussed in the other volumes of the *Basic Computer Series*.

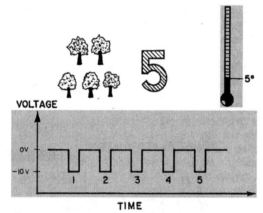

Fig. 1-10. A digital computer uses voltage
pulses to represent numbers.

Comparison

In any control process it is necessary to compare an external condition against the desired condition indicated by the control circuits.

In analog computer circuits (Fig. 1-11A) this is often done by subtraction. That is, the external condition is represented by a voltage which is then electronically subtracted from an internal control voltage. The control circuits modify the external process in some manner until the *difference* between the two voltages is zero (a null point). This is the principle of servo-mechanism operation.

In digital computers (Fig. 1-11B), comparisons are often used to identify data. That is, each piece of data used has a group of

14

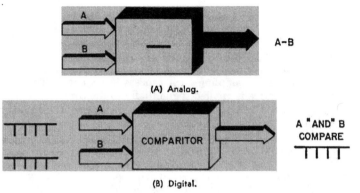

(A) Analog.

(B) Digital.

Fig. 1-11. Examples of computer comparison.

pulses which identify either the source (label) or the destination (address) of the data. The control circuits often compare each pulse in the data label with each pulse in a reference label. When these pulses correspond, the circuits will either route this data to specific destinations in the system or perform operations on it.

Data Transfer

In computers and control systems it is necessary that data be moved from one control circuit to another in the proper se-

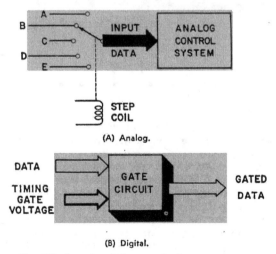

(A) Analog.

(B) Digital.

Fig. 1-12. Examples of data transfer in computers.

quence. In analog systems this may be done by either energizing relays, as in Fig. 1-12A, which transfer data from stage to stage in a fixed sequence, or merely by connecting the stages with wires. When many processes are being controlled, switching must be done by sampling each process in sequence. The data from each source is applied sequentially to the control circuits by means of multi-position stepping switches whose contacts are moved mechanically from one position to the next by electrically actuated mechanisms.

In digital systems, there are many possible operations which can be performed on input data. In the performance of these operations, information is transferred from point to point by data-transfer circuits (gates) which electronically route the signals when a timing-control signal is applied (Fig. 1-12B).

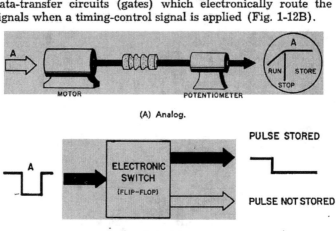

(A) Analog.

(B) Digital.

Fig. 1-13. Examples of data storage in computers.

Data Storage

Analog storage devices often consist of motor-driven potentiometers (Fig. 1-13A), the movable arms of which remain in the last position used when their motors are stopped. These pots can then later provide an output voltage indicating that position. There are other devices that also store analog data, but these will be discussed later.

Digital data (pulses) are "two-value" quantities. A pulse is either yes or no, present or absent, with no in-betweens. The simplest form of digital storage devices are two-position switches or relays in which two fixed DC-voltage levels, as shown in Fig. 1-13B, are used to represent data. When the switch is connected to one voltage level, a pulse is represented. When the switch is connected to the other voltage level, "no" pulse is represented. When the data (from storage) is desired, special circuits convert the DC levels back into "pulses" and "no-pulses." There are also circuits which act like two-position switches (flip-flop) which will be discussed later.

Operation Sequencing and Timing

Mention has been made that certain computer operations occur in fixed sequences. Special circuits are used to cause these operations to occur at specific times.

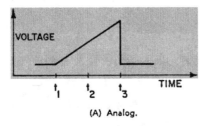

(A) Analog.

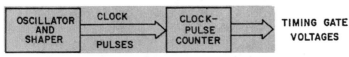

(B) Digital.

Fig. 1-14. Examples of computer sequencing and timing.

Changing voltages, having *magnitudes* equal to an elapsed time, are often used for timing in analog computers (Fig. 1-14A). When sequential switching is used, resistance-inductance (RL) or resistance-capacitance (RC) timing-gate voltages are continuously generated and used to operate stepping switches.

In digital computers, timing and sequencing is controlled by very stable oscillators and pulse counters. The oscillator output is shaped to provide pulses which occur at a uniform repetition rate. The pulse counters count these pulses and indicate how many of them have occurred (Fig. 1-14B). Since this count tells the computer "what time it is," the counters are often called *clocks* and the pulses are often called *clock* or *timing pulses*. The time indications from the counter are represented by timing-control gate voltages which are used to perform sequencing operations. For example, when the clock counter indicates 5 seconds, data is added to other data. When it says 6 sec-

17

onds, the sum is transferred to data storage. When the clock counter says 8 seconds, the stored sum is taken out of storage and added to a new number, etc. Actually, digital computers perform steps in millionths of a second (microseconds) so the clock counters generally indicate time in microseconds.

Yes-No Decision Making

The digital computer has "logic" circuits which can "look at" many conditions (represented by the presence or absence of pulses or DC levels) and make yes-no decisions. The logic circuit indicates a "yes" decision by creating a pulse or DC level. A "no" decision is represented by the absence of a pulse or by a second DC level. *Yes-no decision making is the most important ability of logic circuits.*

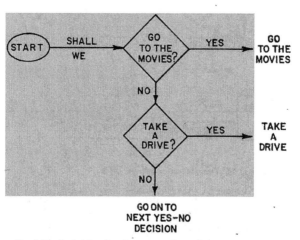

Fig. 1-15. A decision based on a number of yes-no processes.

Many human reasoning processes can be broken down to a long series of yes-no decisions. Fig. 1-15 shows how the next decision in each case depends upon whether the preceding one was "yes" or "no." These same human processes can be simulated by digital-computer logic circuits which say "yes" when *all input conditions are simultaneously present,* or when any *one of a few possible conditions are present.*

Digital computers are *not* "giant brains." Instead, they are machines which have been made to carry out a fixed sequence of yes-no decisions. They can sense the environment (when represented as a group of yes-no condition indications), and can

18

provide one of many *fixed* responses. In this respect they are very ingenious machines.

The decision-making circuits can work tirelessly, doing all sorts of tedious and repetitious jobs. They can sort, collate, do bookkeeping, billing, make up payrolls, guide aircraft, continuously watch and control industrial and chemical processes, route telephone messages, perform traffic control, and do many other jobs that are usually boring to humans.

Data Conversion To Desired Form

In any electronic or electrical system, the outputs must be converted into some useful form. (A high fidelity sound system without a speaker would be useless.) As a result, there are a host of converters used with computers and computer control systems (Fig. 1-16).

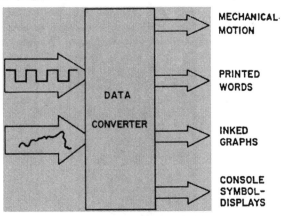

Fig. 1-16. Data conversion is the process of taking computer data and changing it into a useful form.

Analog computers, for example, use motors to provide mechanical action based on the computed results. These motors may operate aircraft controls, move radio and radar antennas, or merely operate an inking pen to record the computed results on a strip of moving paper. Most automation processes are motor-controlled by analog-computer circuits.

Digital computers often use printers that convert the computed data into typed characters on checks, bills, or reports. Digital computers are also used in complex automation systems where the digital output is converted into analog voltages that drive analog motor-control circuits.

19

REVIEW QUESTIONS

1. What is the basic definition of a computer?
2. What is the definition of a Computer Control System?
3. What are the steps of a computer operation?
4. Give some examples of data converters.
5. How are numbers represented in an analog computer?
6. How do digital computers represent numbers?
7. How can the quantity $20y$ be computed, given an analog input voltage of y?
8. How would a digital computer compute the value of 6 times 4?
9. How is operation sequencing and timing used in an automobile?
10. Describe the decision to wear either a raincoat, sunglasses, topcoat, or jacket as a series of yes-no decisions?
11. How does a light bulb satisfy the requirements of an electrical-to-desired-form converter?

CHAPTER 2

Circuits Common to .
Analog and Digital Computers

Circuits common to both analog and digital computers are:

1. Regulated Power Supplies.
2. Emitter Followers.
3. DC Amplifiers.

Regulated voltages are essential for most computers. Input variations in the voltages used to represent numerical quantities in analog computers will result in output errors. Digital circuits will represent false conditions if supply voltages vary excessively or suddenly. Thus well regulated power supplies are necessary for both types of computers.

Emitter followers are primarily used for impedance selection. In analog computers, the input impedance of the high-gain DC amplifiers used for computing must be very high to assure proper circuit operation. In digital computers, there are severe loading effects caused by several circuits being driven by a common signal source. In this case, emitter followers are used as high-impedance loads to isolate the various circuits from the source. In this application the emitter follower is used as a power amplifier as well as a high load resistance.

DC (direct-coupled) amplifiers are used in both analog and digital computers. This type of amplifier is capable of processing signals which remain fairly constant over relatively long periods of time. Any type of capacitive or inductive coupling between amplifier stages would pass only changing signals. The DC amplifier is capable of processing both DC and fairly high-frequency signals. This results in a pass band extending from zero cycles (DC) up into the megacycle region.

REGULATED POWER SUPPLIES

All power supplies have an internal resistance which will cause their output voltage to vary as changes in output current

21

or in the input AC voltage occur. A regulated power supply has an added resistance which is automatically varied to maintain a constant output voltage for moderate variations in input voltage or output current.

A regulated power supply consists of three basic elements:

1. Rectifier.
2. Control circuit.
3. Regulator.

In most cases, all of these elements contain semiconductor devices. Semiconductor diodes are used in the rectifier, and transistors in the control circuit and regulator.

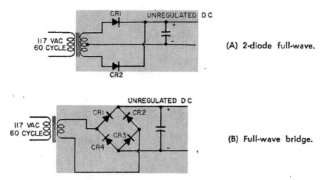

Fig. 2-1. Typical rectifier circuits used in transistor power supplies.

The rectifier provides unregulated, filtered DC. The regulator is a transistor connected either in series with the rectifier voltage or across the rectifier output terminals.

The control circuit samples the output voltage and varies the resistance of the regulator transistor when the rectifier output voltage varies from the desired value. The ripple voltage from the rectifier is virtually eliminated by the regulator.

The Rectifier

Full-wave, capacitively-filtered rectifiers (Fig. 2-1) are usually used. The rectifier may use either two diodes or a bridge of four diodes. In the two-diode rectifier, either CR1 or CR2 conducts depending upon the instantaneous polarity of the sine wave across the transformer secondary. In the bridge rectifier, CR1 and CR3 conduct when the voltage at the top of the secondary is positive. CR2 and CR4 conduct when the voltage at that point is negative.

22

Step-down transformers are used to provide transistor supply voltages from 3 to 50 volts. The current capacity of the transformer is determined by the number of transistors to be driven. A few amperes of current are usually required. In large computer installations, however, many power supplies are used to furnish total currents in the order of hundreds of amperes.

The Control Circuit and Regulator

The control circuit is a device which compares the rectifier output voltage with a desired reference voltage. A difference between the two voltages causes the control circuit to vary the base current to the regulator transistor. This, in turn, causes the transistor resistance to vary. As a result, the voltage drop

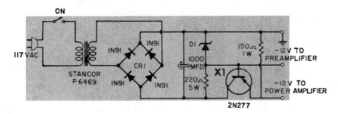

DI-INI524A ZENER DIODE, I2V, I WATT

Fig. 2-2. 12-volt, 1-ampere regulated power supply.

across or the current drawn by the transistor varies. This variation causes the power-supply output voltage to be either reduced or increased.

An Example of a Series Regulator. A simple regulated power supply (Fig. 2-2) uses a zener diode and a resistor for the control circuit and a *series* transistor for the regulator. Transistor X1 and resistor R2 form a voltage divider. The main power-supply output voltage is developed across resistor R2. The resistance of transistor X1, which affects the output voltage, is controlled by the base current.

When the voltage divider is perfectly balanced, the voltage developed across resistor R2 is −12 volts and the voltage developed across transistor X1 is approximately −22 volts. A base-to-emitter voltage of a few tenths of a volt exists and causes a small base current to flow.

The voltage developed across diode CR2 is applied directly to the base of transistor X1. Diode CR2 is a zener diode. As you recall, a zener diode breaks down when reverse biased and maintains a fixed voltage within fairly wide ranges of current.

23

The zener diode used in this circuit provides a fixed reference voltage of −12 volts.

The base-to-emitter voltage applied to transistor X1 consists of the *difference* between the zener-diode reference voltage and the power-supply output voltage. Since the reference voltage is constant, changes in output voltage cause the transistor base-to-emitter voltage to change, and consequently the base current to vary.

Suppose, for example, the rectifier voltage increased (became more negative) due to an increase in the AC-input voltage. The increased voltage across transistor X1 and resistor R2 would cause the output voltage to begin to rise. However, as soon as the output voltage rises a few hundredths of a volt, the base-to-emitter voltage decreases by the same amount. This very small decrease in base-to-emitter voltage reduces the base current. The high current gain of the transistor results in this small base-current decrease causing a much larger decrease in collector current and a relatively large increase in collector-to-emitter resistance. Consequently, the output voltage increases only a few hundredths of a volt, with the remainder of the rectifier voltage increase being developed across the increased collector-to-emitter resistance of transistor X1.

On the other hand, when the rectifier voltage is reduced, or when an increased load current causes the output voltage to drop a few hundredths of a volt, the increase in base current causes the transistor resistance to decrease. Consequently, a greater portion of the rectifier voltage is developed across the output resistance.

Of course, resistor R2 is actually in parallel with the resistance of the circuits being supplied by the power supply. Hence, the resistance in series with transistor X1 consists of the parallel combination of R2 and the load resistance. However, the output voltage of the power supply varies by only 2% from no-current load to the full-current load of 1 ampere. In addition, the voltage ripple of the rectifier is reduced to 0.1% of the output voltage by the regulation process.

Also note that the reference voltage developed across the zener diode is used as a low-power voltage supply. This arrangement is very similar to that used with a gas-filled regulator tube. Resistor R1 limits the current flowing in the zener diode.

An Example of a Shunt Regulator. The shunt regulator (Fig. 2-3) uses a regulator transistor connected *across* (in shunt) the rectifier output. In this arrangement the regulated output voltage is developed across the shunt transistor.

24

Increases in rectifier-input voltage result in increased base voltage since the zener voltage is constant. As a result, increased collector current flows, the collector-to-emitter resistance decreases, and the output voltage decreases to the desired value. The increased collector current causes a larger voltage to be developed across R1. The emitter-voltage increase, however, does not exceed the base voltage and the transistor remains conducting more heavily.

Decreases in output voltage cause the emitter voltage to approach the base voltage and hence cause less base-current flow. The decreased base-current flow decreases the collector current and causes the output voltage to increase.

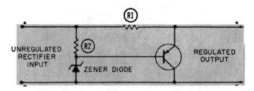

Fig. 2-3. A shunt-regulator configuration.

The current-handling capability of the shunt- or series-regulated power supply can be extended through the use of parallel transistors. In this arrangement, each regulator transistor carries a portion of the total supply current. The resistive power losses associated with the regulator transistors become excessive, however, when high currents are regulated.

Pulse-Regulated Power Supplies

High-current power supplies often make use of pulse techniques in order to reduce the power loss associated with series or shunt regulators. Pulsed power supplies have efficiencies close to 100%. This means that almost no power is lost in converting the AC into DC. In high-current supplies using other methods of conversion, as much as 50% of the input power is wasted in heat dissipation by the resistive elements.

In the pulsed power supply, short bursts of power are applied to an LC filter which provides stable DC. The width (in time) of these pulses determine the DC output of the power supply.

The Silicon Controlled-Rectifier. The basic element of the pulsed power supply is a device called a silicon controlled-rectifier (SCR). The SCR is essentially a gated diode and is designed so that a high-AC input voltage alone is not sufficient to cause forward conduction. For example, a General Electric

25

C35H SCR will not conduct even when there is a forward voltage of 165 volts across it. However, when a narrow 3-volt gate pulse is applied to the SCR cathode, conduction occurs. Even after the gate pulse is removed, this conduction continues until reverse bias is applied. After the SCR is reverse biased, it regains its forward-blocking ability in approximately 20 microseconds (recovery time).

The circuit configuration of a pulse-regulated power supply (Fig. 2-4) consists of a gated bridge-rectifier containing silicon controlled-rectifiers, a filter, a voltage-sensor circuit and a control circuit.

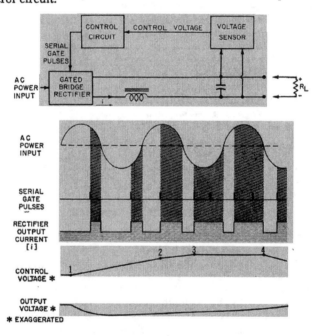

Fig. 2-4. A pulse-regulated power supply.

Pulses of voltage and current are applied to the filter by the gated bridge-rectifier. The voltage developed across the capacitor is a DC voltage proportional to the average value of the full-wave pulses of current. This average value increases as the width of the pulses increase. The inductor attenuates the AC components of the pulses.

The value of the output voltage is sampled by the voltage sensor which controls the frequency of the serial gate-pulses provided by the control circuit. When the output voltage falls below the desired value, the control voltage causes the gate pulses to occur at a high frequency. As a result, the gated bridge-rectifier is gated on earlier in the AC input-voltage cycle. This causes a wider voltage and current pulse to occur. The wider voltage and current pulses have a high average value, and hence cause the output voltage developed across the capacitor to increase. When the output voltage returns to the preset value, the voltage sensor provides a control voltage sufficient to maintain the output voltage constant.

When the output voltage goes above the desired value, the control voltage causes the frequency of the gate pulses to de-

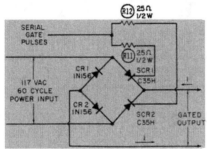

Fig. 2-5. A gated bridge-rectifier.

crease. This causes the rectifier current pulses to become narrower and thus results in a smaller output voltage.

Gated Bridge-Rectifier. The gated bridge-rectifier (Fig. 2-5) consists of two normal diodes, CR1 and CR2, and two silicon controlled-rectifiers, SCR1 and SCR2. Resistors R11 and R12 limit the current drawn by the cathodes of the SCR's.

When a gate pulse is applied, the SCR which is forward biased conducts. It continues to conduct (even after the gate pulse is removed) until the polarity of the AC input reverses. This behavior is similar to that of a thyratron. Diode CR2 conducts and provides a return path for current flowing through SCR1. Diode CR1 provides the return path for SCR2.

The voltage sensor (Fig. 2-6) provides a control voltage of opposite direction to the variation of the output voltage. That is, when the output voltage of the power supply decreases the transistor conduction is reduced (because the base becomes less positive with respect to the emitter) and the sensor output voltage rises. On the other hand, when the power-supply output voltage increases, the transistor conduction is increased and the sensor output voltage decreases.

27

The base-to-emitter voltage of transistor X1 is determined by the setting of potentiometer R1. The emitter voltage is held constant by zener diode CR5. Potentiometer R1 is adjusted so that the base voltage is slightly positive with respect to the emitter.

The amount of collector current flowing as a result of the setting of potentiometer R1 will determine the normal value of the control-voltage output of the sensor. As mentioned previously, this control voltage will affect the frequency of the serial

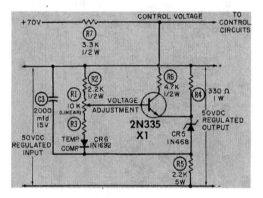

Fig. 2-6. A voltage sensor.

gate-pulses. Thus, this setting also affects the value of the power-supply output voltage.

Diode CR6 provides temperature compensation for the voltage sensor. The diode has a forward resistance which varies with temperature. As ambient temperature increases, additional and undesirable collector current increases. This same temperature increase causes the forward resistance of diode CR6 to decrease. This, in turn, causes the base voltage of transistor X1 to become lower and hence reduces the collector current to the desired value. Capacitor C3 bypasses transient current pulses that occur during normal operating or during power supply turn-on and turn-off intervals. Resistor R5 provides a common voltage-dropping resistor for zener diode CR5 and the transistor base-current voltage divider. Resistors R6 and R7 form a voltage divider which provides an output voltage of the desired magnitude.

The Control Circuit. The circuit shown in Fig. 2-7 is a relaxation oscillator that is identical, functionally, to a thyratron relaxation oscillator. The main element of the oscillator is the

28

unijunction transistor X2. This transistor conducts heavily when the input voltage exceeds a fixed value.

In the circuit shown, transistor X2 will conduct when capacitor C1 charges to the firing voltage. The resulting conduction current allows capacitor C1 to discharge through resistor R10. This produces one of the serial gate-pulses for the gated rectifier.

The frequency of the serial gate-pulses depends upon the time that it takes for capacitor C1 to charge to the firing volt-

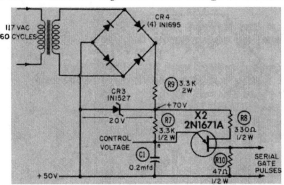

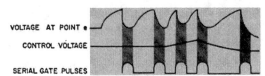

Fig. 2-7. Control circuit.

age. This time depends, in turn, on the DC voltage applied at point e by the control voltage. That is, the capacitor will charge and discharge from that voltage. Looking at it from another point of view, the control voltage is the DC level around which the capacitor voltage varies. The higher the DC level, the faster will be the triggering rate, because the capacitor doesn't have to charge very much in order to fire the transistor.

The basic frequency of oscillation is determined by the values of C1 and R7. Diodes CR4, resistor R9, and zener diode CR3, form a power supply for the oscillator. The voltage developed across CR3 is a full-wave unfiltered voltage, clipped to an amplitude of 20 volts.

The complete pulse-regulated power supply (Fig. 2-8) merely consists of the functional elements that have been discussed.

29

Note that diode CR7 provides a discharge path for the current associated with the voltage induced in inductor, L, when the power supply is de-energized. The diode also discharges filter capacitor C2 to a certain extent during the conduction interval.

The supply shown provides 50 volts at a current of 10 amperes. The output voltage varies by only ½% over a wide range of load currents and input voltages.

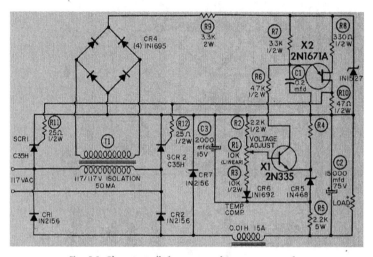

Fig. 2-8. Phase-controlled constant-voltage power supply.

EMITTER FOLLOWERS

Emitter followers are often used in transistorized analog and digital circuits because of the high input and low output impedance that they provide.

The basic emitter follower (Fig. 2-9) consists of a transistor having a single resistor in the emitter circuit. The input impedance is approximately equal to βR_E or $H_{FE} R_E$.

The large difference between the ohmic value of emitter resistance and the input impedance occurs because of the collector current flowing through R_E. The collector current develops a fairly large voltage drop across the emitter resistance. As a result, the base-to-emitter voltage is quite a bit smaller than the voltage applied to the base by the preceding circuit. That is, the base-to-emitter voltage is the *difference* between the base

30

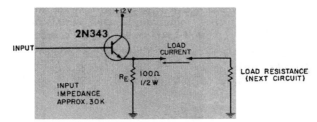

Fig. 2-9. A basic emitter-follower.

voltage and the emitter voltage. The input current is then reduced because of the reduced voltage across the base-emitter junction.

The major disadvantage of the basic emitter-follower is that variations in load current and load resistance change the voltage developed across the emitter resistance and hence vary the input impedance. These load-resistance variations occur because the input impedance of other transistor-circuit configurations are functions of the collector current flowing in these circuits.

Input-impedance variations of the basic emitter-follower can be virtually eliminated by adding collector resistance (Fig. 2-10). Note that the emitter resistance has been increased in order to offset the loss of emitter voltage caused by the addition of the collector resistor. The 150K resistor is used for bias stabilization. Also note that this circuit was expressly designed for use with negative pulses. A circuit designed to process sine-waves, for example, would be slightly different.

Other High-input-Impedance Circuits

An obvious method of creating a high input impedance is to use a high resistance in series with the base of a transistor

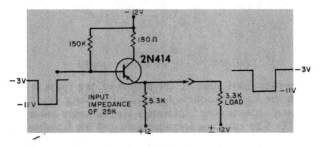

Fig. 2-10. A modified emitter-follower.

31

(Fig. 2-11). The disadvantage of this system is that minor variations in series-resistor value causes small variations in base current which are amplified and cause larger variations in collector current. However, the circuit shown is intended for use with digital circuits where large values of base current are used and minor variations do not appreciably affect the collector current.

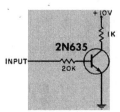

Fig. 2-11. A high impedance at the input results from using a resistance in series with the base.

Other methods of creating a high input impedance are also used. Most of them, however, are not suitable for use in direct-coupled circuits. The reasons for this are discussed in the next topic.

DIRECT-COUPLED (DC) AMPLIFIERS

The wide range of frequencies and pulse repetition rates encountered in analog and digital circuits make it necessary to use a coupling method which is not frequency sensitive. This method is direct coupling.

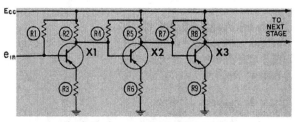

Fig. 2-12. An example of direct coupling.

In direct-coupled circuits, the output of one stage is fed directly to the next. Frequency-sensitive coupling devices such as blocking capacitors and interstage transformers are not used (Fig. 2-12). The coupling arrangements and the function of the components will be discussed in the sections dealing with specific analog and digital circuits.

32

REVIEW QUESTIONS

1. Why are regulated power supplies used in computer circuits?

2. How are emitter followers used in computer circuits?

3. Why are direct-coupled amplifiers used in computers?

4. Name two types of full-wave rectifiers.

5. What are the three elements of a regulated power supply?

6. How does a series regulator work?

7. How does a shunt regulator work?

8. Why are pulse-regulated power supplies used?

9. How do pulse-regulated power supplies work?

10. How are emitter followers affected by variations in load resistance?

11. How is the variation in emitter-follower input resistance reduced?

12. What is the main circuit characteristic of direct-coupled stages?

33

CHAPTER 3

Analog Computers

The analog computer uses voltages to represent numerical quantities and mathematical operations are performed on these voltages by electronic circuits. This portion of the book deals with the transistorized circuits used to perform these mathematical operations.

Analog-computer circuits are used to:

1. Control industrial processes.
2. Imitate (simulate) the behavior of equipment being designed or analyzed.
3. Compute navigational data and guide aircraft and missiles.
4. Solve scientific equations.
5. Compute positional data and guide large guns or radar antennas.
6. Provide data displays for data-processing systems.
7. Process medical data for measuring devices connected to human beings.
8. Process data for telemetering and remote-control systems.
9. Guide machine tools from instructions on a magnetic tape.

All of these applications are accomplished using converters and operational amplifiers. These operational amplifiers are connected in various ways in order to perform mathematical operations.

OPERATIONAL AMPLIFIER CHARACTERISTICS

As mentioned before, the major circuit of the analog computer is the operational amplifier. Transistorized versions of operational amplifiers must provide the same operating capabilities as the vacuum-tube counterpart. The amplifier must provide:

35

1. Voltage gains in the order of 15,000 to 30,000 or higher.
2. Faithful reproduction of signal waveforms.
3. High input impedance.
4. Freedom from drift.

The behavior of the operational amplifier is influenced very strongly by externally-connected circuits. That is, a single operational amplifier can be externally connected to invert, add, subtract, multiply by a constant, or integrate. The behavior of the amplifier will depend entirely on the external circuit.

When used with electronic or servo multipliers, the operational amplifier can square quantities and take square roots. A combined system using many operational amplifiers and multipliers can perform almost any mathematical operation.

Function of the Operational Amplifier

It is possible to perform mathematical operations using passive components such as resistors and capacitors. However,

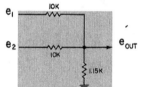

Fig. 3-1. A passive adder.

when such components are used, problems arise which can only be solved by operational amplifiers. For example, when resistors are used to add or subtract (Fig. 3-1) the voltages applied to both inputs cause a current to flow in the common resistor. Ideally, this current represents the sum of the two voltages applied to the adder. However, there is a problem involved. The adder also acts as a voltage divider. That is, only one-tenth of the sum of the two input voltages appears at the output.

The most obvious answer to this problem is to apply the output voltage to an amplifier having a gain of 10. Thus, the true sum of the input voltages would appear at the amplifier output. The main requirements of this amplifier are:

1. That it provide a very stable low gain.
2. That it does not draw excessive current from the adder circuit (have high input impedance).
3. That it faithfully reproduces the input waveforms (have wide-frequency response).
4. That it responds to small signals (have high sensitivity).

These requirements are all met by a feedback amplifier. A feedback amplifier is constructed by designing a high-gain amplifier and using negative feedback to produce stable low gain and wide-frequency response. In addition, direct coupling (DC) is used so that the amplifier also responds to direct-current voltages. The operational amplifier is a high-gain DC amplifier. The external circuits mentioned previously provide the required negative feedback.

Collector-to-Base Negative Feedback. The negative feedback used with operational amplifiers is slightly different than the conventional current or voltage feedback. The method used has formally been called plate-to-grid feedback. In the case of transistors, however, the term collector-to-base feedback would be more appropriate.

Collector-to-base feedback (Fig. 3-2) consists of connecting an amplifier output (the collector) through a feedback resistor

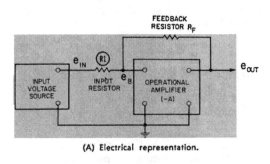

(A) Electrical representation.

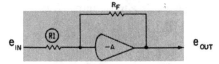

(B) Symbolic representation.

Fig. 3-2. Collector-to-base feedback.

back to the input (the base). In addition, an input resistor is also used. As a result, the amplifier output voltage causes a current to flow through the input source (input resistor) and the feedback resistor. The feedback is negative because the output voltage fed back is always 180 degrees out-of-phase with the input.

The operation of the circuit is such that the output voltage always assumes a value which causes the voltage at the *amplifier* input to be reduced to almost zero. The amplifier output

37

voltage may be positive or negative depending on the biasing arrangement used in the output stage. The value of output voltage required to null the *amplifier* input voltage is an amplified and inverted version of the *circuit* input voltage.

From a current-flow point of view, the amplifier output voltage causes a current to flow through the input resistance. This current develops a voltage across the input resistance which is of opposite polarity to the input voltage. As a result, the total voltage between the *amplifier* input and ground is almost zero. This point is often called a *virtual ground* because the voltage there is always very close to zero.

The gain of the operational amplifier is so large that a relatively small input voltage causes much larger output voltages. For example, an input of 0.001 volts will provide an output of 30 volts when the amplifier has a gain of 30,000.

The value of the operational-amplifier output voltage is determined by the values of feedback and input resistance. The gain with feedback is:

$$A_F = -\frac{R_F}{R_I}$$

Note that the gain of the circuit is independent of the amplifier gain. This will only be true when the amplifier gain is in the order of 15,000 to 30,000 or higher.

The gain equation is very simply derived. All that must be remembered is that the current that flows in the input resistor is the same current that flows in the feedback resistor (the current drawn by the amplifier must be negligible) and that the *amplifier* input voltage, e_B, is almost zero. Thus:

$$i_{in} = i_F; \quad \frac{e_B - e_{in}}{R_I} = \frac{e_o - e_B}{R_F}$$

Since

$$e_B \approx 0, \text{ then } \frac{-e_{in}}{R_I} = \frac{e_o}{R_F}$$

Rearranging terms:

$$\frac{e_o}{e_{in}} = -\frac{R_F}{R_I} = A_F$$

It is important to note that it can only be assumed that e_B is nearly zero when the gain of the amplifier is very, very large.

Operational Amplifier Adders

In the discussion of the function of operational amplifiers it was shown how an adder could be constructed using resistors.

38

At that time the only interest was in a stable amplifier. It turns out, however, that the operational amplifier can be used as an adder also (Fig. 3-3). The same principles of collector-to-base feedback also apply in this case. In the adder circuit, the total

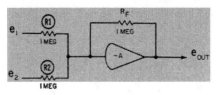

Fig. 3-3. An operational-amplifier adder.

current flowing through the feedback resistor consists of the sum of the two currents flowing through the input resistors. Thus:

$$i_F = i_1 + i_2$$

and:

$$\frac{e_o - e_B}{R_F} = \frac{e_B - e_1}{R_1} + \frac{e_B - e_2}{R_2}$$

Since

$$e_B \approx 0, \text{ then } \frac{e_o}{R_F} = \frac{-e_1}{R_1} - \frac{e_2}{R_2}$$

Rearranging terms:

$$e_o = -e_1 \left(\frac{R_F}{R_1}\right) - e_2 \left(\frac{R_F}{R_2}\right)$$

In the circuit shown,

$$\frac{R_F}{R} = 1.$$

Thus:

$$e_o = -(e_1 + e_2)$$

REVIEW QUESTIONS

1. List some applications of analog computer circuits.

2. What are the requirements for an analog computer amplifier?

3. What type of amplifier satisfies the requirements for an analog computer amplifier?

4. What is the gain of an operational amplifier with external resistance feedback?

5. What is the output voltage of an adder circuit?

39

CHAPTER 4

Operational Amplifiers

Now that some uses of the operational amplifier have been discussed, the circuits themselves will be considered.

The basic circuits employed are fairly simple. They consist of a series of directly-coupled transistorized class-A amplifiers. However, certain other circuits and networks are also used for reasons which will now be discussed.

DRIFT VOLTAGES AND THE
DIFFERENCE AMPLIFIER

The first few stages in any type of high-gain amplifier are always a problem. The most insignificant variations in quiescent output voltage can be disastrous when they are amplified, and thus multiplied, 20,000 times or so. In DC amplifiers these variations are not blocked by coupling capacitors and are definitely noticed at the output. These variations, called drift voltages, occur in transistors as a result of:

1. Variations in power-supply voltages.
2. Changes in transistor gain due to temperature variations.
3. Changes in transistor quiescent current due to temperature variations.
4. Thermal-noise voltages.
5. Changes in transistor base-to-emitter voltage as a result of temperature variations.

As can be seen, change in characteristics due to temperature variation is the main cause of drift in transistorized DC amplifiers. In many cases, the drift voltage (when amplified) would be enough to drive the last few stages into current saturation. Fortunately, circuits are available which considerably reduce these drift voltages.

The most widely used drift-reduction circuit is the difference amplifier (Fig. 4-1). As the name implies, the output voltage

41

(taken between collectors) is equal to the difference between the two input voltages. Any variations in output, caused by drift voltages, is cancelled because both transistors are almost equally affected and the difference voltage between collectors remains constant.

The circuit can be used with either two inputs or with one having a fixed bias. In either case, collector current drawn by one transistor effects that drawn by the other. This occurs because of the common emitter resistor.

An increase in the collector current of transistor X1, for example, increases the emitter voltage of transistor X2. However, the base-to-emitter voltage of transistor X2 will be decreased

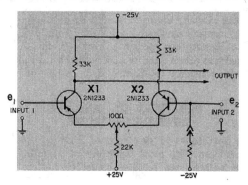

Fig. 4-1. A basic transistorized difference amplifier.

(if the base voltage is held constant) since the *difference* between the base voltage and the emitter voltage appears there. Consequently, the base current of transistor X2 decreases and the collector voltage increases. Since the collector voltage of transistor X1 decreases, the difference voltage becomes greater.

The difference amplifier provides a gain determined by the common-emitter, small-signal current gain of each stage. The equation that describes this operation is rather involved. By physical reasoning, however, it can be seen that as one collector voltage is reduced, the other collector voltage is increased. The difference voltage between the two collectors is much greater than the difference between the two input voltages because of the current gain of the two transistors. The high value of emitter resistance and voltage also provides a very high input impedance.

The potentiometer in the emitter circuit is used to adjust the circuit output voltage when no input is present. That is, by

42

varying the emitter voltages of the two transistors it is possible to select the values of quiescent base currents.

DC AMPLIFIERS

A typical DC amplifier (Fig. 4-2) consists of a few difference-amplifier stages and a few stages of conventional amplification. Negative feedback is used within the amplifier to provide stable gains over a wide range of frequencies. These frequencies are often the component frequencies of step voltages, pulses, ramp or sawtooth voltages, and the transient conditions associated with the sudden application of AC signals. In some applications,

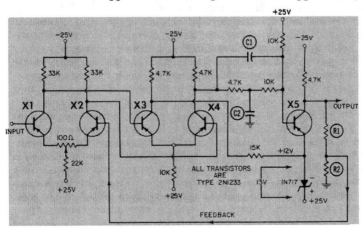

Fig. 4-2. A typical DC amplifier.

the input signals are combinations of some of the above mentioned waveforms.

In negative feedback circuits, a fixed portion (percentage) of the output voltage is fed back to the input and used to cancel out a portion of the input voltage or current. In some ways, the feedback circuit consisting of R1 and R2 appears similar to the collector-to-base negative feedback discussed earlier. However, the way in which the feedback operates is quite different.

A fixed portion of the overall output voltage (developed by the R1 and R2 voltage divider) is fed back to transistor X2. The base current caused by this voltage is amplified and affects the emitter voltage of transistor X1. The voltage fed back to transistor X2 is in phase with the input voltage. However, since transistors X1 and X2 form a difference amplifier, the output

43

is an amplified version of the instantaneous algebraic difference between the two input currents. That is, the feedback voltage will cause a feedback current that will subtract from, or cancel, the effect of the input current.

The feedback voltage thus effectively changes the gain of the first stage. In other words, the effect of reducing the input current by cancellation is the same as would be obtained by leaving the input current alone and lowering the gain of the stage. On the other hand, if the feedback decreases, less of the input current is cancelled and the effective stage gain is increased.

In addition, the gain of the first stage can be made different for different frequency components of the same signal. For example, suppose that the amplification of a high-frequency component of an input signal was reduced because of attenuation caused by shunt capacitance in the circuits. The output waveform would tend to become distorted. However, *that* frequency component of the input will not undergo as much cancellation at the difference-amplifier input as the other frequency components and hence will appear at the output with a slightly higher amplitude.

Note that a small fraction of a volt of feedback is sufficient to provide the base current required to cause a rather large amplifier-output voltage. As a result, an extremely small variation in output voltage, caused by amplifier attenuation of a frequency component, is quite enough to cause the feedback circuit to compensate for the change and keep the *effective* amplifier gain almost constant for a wide range of frequency components.

To function properly, the feedback and the output voltage of the overall amplifier must be exactly in phase with the input voltage and current.

Unfortunately, however, the input capacitances of each stage introduce time delays or phase shifts. These phase shifts depend upon the frequency components of the signal passing through the amplifier. Without some form of compensation, distortion would be produced as a result of subtracting two current waveforms that are not exactly in phase.

The resistor-capacitor network applying base current to transistor X5 provides the extra phase shift required to make the output voltage exactly in phase with the input voltage and current.

A plot of frequency-versus-phase shift for the network would show (when proper values of C1 and C2 were selected) a phase-shift characteristic exactly opposite to the uncompensated phase-shift characteristics of the amplifier. As a result, the phase shifts introduced in the amplifier are cancelled by the network. The values of C1 and C2 are dictated by the phase shifts produced by the circuit and by the frequency range.

The circuit shown (Fig. 4-2) receives input current at the base of transistor X1 and feedback current at the base of transistor X2. The biasing arrangement used on all stages cause the output voltages to vary around a reference voltage of zero. The output voltages can be either positive or negative.

It was noted earlier that applying in-phase voltages to a difference amplifier produced an amplified voltage proportional to the difference between the two inputs. By the same token, the two 180-degree out-of-phase inputs applied to the difference amplifier, composed of transistors X3 and X4, produces an amplified output proportional to the sum of the inputs applied to the bases.

Note that the collector and emitter resistance of the second stage is considerably less than that of the first. The reduced resistance allows a much greater collector current to flow, and hence provides greater collector-voltage variations. That is, the output voltages of the second stage will be considerably higher than those of the first.

The common-emitter resistances of the difference amplifier stages provide very high input impedances. The input impedance of the first stage is in the order of 100,000 ohms.

Note the arrangement used to supply the base-to-emitter current for transistor X5. Here, the output voltages of transistors X3 and X4 cause a base-to-emitter current flow.

The emitter of transistor X5 is held to a +12 volts by the combination of the +25-volt supply and the −13-volt zener diode (type 1N717). As a result, the collector of transistor X3 draws a current through the base-emitter junction of transistor X5 without changing the emitter voltage. The resistor in series with the output of transistor X3 limits the current drawn by the base-emitter circuit of transistor X4.

The 10K resistor connected between the base of transistor X5 and the +25-volt supply provides bias current. The arrangement causes a voltage of very slightly less than +12 volts to appear at the base of X5 when no signal is present. Since the emitter is at +12 volts, a small bias current flows through the base-to-emitter junction.

The portion of the output voltage developed across resistor R2 is used as the feedback voltage for transistor X2. When the values of R1 and R2 are chosen to provide a feedback voltage equal to 1 percent of the output voltage, an overall stable voltage gain of 100 results. Resistors of 4.7K and 470K can be used

45

to provide a good approximation of the 1 percent feedback voltage.

The potentiometer between the emitters of transistors X1 and X2 is adjusted to provide an overall output of zero volts when no input is present. Higher gains are achieved by adding additional stages of amplification.

HIGH-GAIN OPERATIONAL AMPLIFIERS

The DC amplifier previously discussed had a voltage gain of 100. Now a higher-gain circuit will be discussed.

The block diagram of an amplifier capable of supplying a voltage gain of 25,000 is shown in Fig. 4-3. Note that this am-

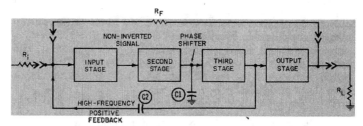

Fig. 4-3. Block diagram of a high-gain operational amplifier.

plifier uses a single capacitor (C1) for phase-shift correction. In addition, a special positive-feedback path is provided for the higher-frequency components of the input signal. Note also, that the output of the third stage is in phase with the input because the input stage does not invert the signal.

External-feedback resistors are also shown. The gain, with feedback, can be varied from 1 (input resistor of 4.7K and feedback resistance of 4.7K) to 10 (input resistor of 4.7K and feedback resistance of 47K). Higher gains are accomplished using higher values of feedback resistance. In most analog-computer applications, however, a gain of 10 is sufficient. The maximum output voltage is plus or minus 5 volts, feeding into a load resistance of 1,500 ohms.

The Input Stage

The input stage (Fig. 4-4) is a grounded-collector amplifier (emitter follower). The voltage divider in the collector circuit provides a small negative voltage for the collector of the transistor. This voltage, approximately −0.8 volts, allows the output of the stage to assume small negative values. The input volt-

46

ages range from zero to plus or minus 0.0002 volts. As a result, the output voltage of the first stage is in this range.

The resistor from the base to ground is in parallel with the stage input resistance. The unshunted input resistance of the stage is considerably higher than 50K. However, this input resistance is not a constant quantity, but varies considerably as a result of the different currents drawn by the following stage. That is, the collector current varies as a function of emitter resistance and is not absolutely constant.

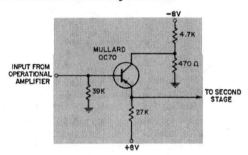

Fig. 4-4. An emitter-follower input stage.

The shunt resistor is small with respect to the unshunted input resistance. As a result, the unshunted input resistance can vary widely without seriously affecting the combined parallel resistance consisting of the shunt resistor and the unshunted input resistance. In addition, the shunt resistor reduces variation in the output resistance of the stage due to variations in the resistance of the input-signal source.

The Second Stage

The second stage (Fig. 4-5) is a straight-forward common-emitter amplifier. The 33-ohm resistor in the emitter circuit develops the bias voltage for the stage. That is, the voltage-divider network causes the emitter junction to be positive with respect to the base. This results in the flow of a small bias current.

Also note that the 33-ohm resistor causes a negative feedback to occur in the second stage. Although this feedback reduces stage gain, it also provides wide-frequency response and reduces noise, drift, and other undesirable effects.

The Third Stage and The Output Stage

The third stage and the output stage (Fig. 4-6) are both high-gain, common-emitter amplifiers. Emitter resistors are used to

47

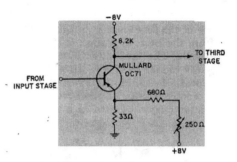

Fig. 4-5. An emitter-follower second stage.

provide self bias. Positive feedback is used in these stages to offset the negative feedback introduced by the emitter resistors. The positive feedback is obtained by feeding a portion of the voltage developed across the collector resistors to the emitter. The emitter of the output stage also receives a bias voltage as a result of a series resistor connected to the positive-voltage supply.

The Complete High-Gain Operational Amplifier

The complete high-gain operational amplifier is shown in Fig. 4-7. Note how the output voltage of each stage varies around a bias voltage developed through the use of voltage-divider networks. Also note how the use of a positive- and a negative-voltage supply makes it possible for the output of each stage to assume positive or negative values.

Operational Considerations. Consider some of the operating conditions dictated by the circuit shown. The maximum allowable output voltage is plus or minus 5 volts. Since the circuit

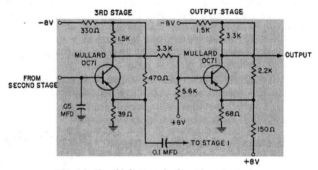

Fig. 4-6. The third stage feeding the output stage.

48

voltage gain is 25,000, this means that the input signal should not exceed plus or minus 0.0002 volts (0.2 millivolts). When the circuit is used as a straight amplifier, the gain is quite sufficient for use with any low-level transducer or data converter.

When used as an operational amplifier, observe the following restrictions:

1. The gain with feedback $\left(\dfrac{R_F}{R_I}\right)$ should never produce an output greater than 5 volts. The gain used and the value of input voltage must be considered.

2. The input resistor should be small compared with the input resistance of the operational amplifier. This limits the value of the input resistor to about 5K (one-tenth of the input resistance). The feedback resistor can be any desired value.

3. The input resistance of the following stage must be 1,500 ohms or higher.

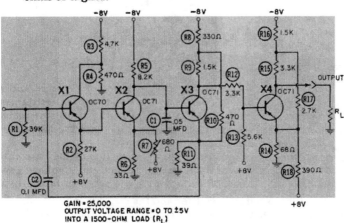

GAIN = 25,000
OUTPUT VOLTAGE RANGE = 0 TO ±5V
INTO A 1500-OHM LOAD (R_L)

Fig. 4-7. A complete high-gain operational amplifier.

TRANSISTORIZED DC-AMPLIFIER ANALYSIS

There are many factors which affect the operation of transistorized DC amplifiers. The relationship between these factors must be understood to use, design, repair, or evaluate the performance of these circuits.

Equivalent-Circuit Analysis

The most straight-forward approach to determining the relationships in an electronic circuit is to develop an equivalent

49

circuit. These equivalent circuits use resistances and voltage generators to represent the transistor. Externally-connected components are also shown.

The equivalent circuit shows all DC power supplies as short circuits. This is done because only the AC components of a signal are considered. This is a reasonable assumption since most electronic power supplies contain filter capacitors designed to short out AC. Batteries represent only a small series resistance to AC.

In a sense, the DC power supplies are indicated by the AC generators used to represent the amplifying properties of the

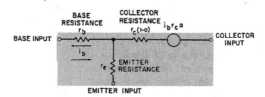

Fig. 4-8. A transistor small-signal equivalent circuit.

transistor. The actual currents and voltages occur as a result of the DC power supplies.

A transistor can be represented in terms of resistors and a voltage generator (Fig. 4-8). The base and emitter resistances essentially represent ohmic resistance of the transistor material. It must also be remembered, however, that the base-emitter junction has the properties of a diode.

The collector resistance varies as a function of the base current and is represented by a fixed resistance and a voltage generator having an output voltage that is a function of the base current (in the common-emitter and the common-collector connection). The value of this equivalent voltage is greater than the base current by a factor of r_c times a. This factor represents the amplifying properties of the transistor.

Actually, the equivalent voltage generator really describes the effect of the changing collector resistance, which varies as a result of base-emitter current flow, developing a varying voltage across it. This voltage is a result of the DC-supply current flowing through the collector resistance. Using this basic equivalent circuit the equivalent circuits for the common-emitter and the common-collector configurations can be developed.

The Common-Emitter Equivalent Circuit. The common-emitter equivalent circuit is derived by adding a load resistor R_L (Fig. 4-9) and by considering the input signal source. The load resistor shown represents the collector load resistance *in parallel with* the input resistance of the following stage.

The factors which affect each stage of a common-emitter DC amplifier are indicated in the equations which describe input resistance, voltage gain, and output resistance.

Consider the input resistance. How can the input resistance of a common-emitter DC amplifier be varied? The answer to this question is found in the equation:

$$R_i = \frac{e_i}{i_b} = r_b + \frac{r_e \, (r_c + R_L)}{r_c \, (1 - a) + r_e + R_L}$$

The most obvious way to vary the input resistance to the stage is to add series resistance in the base circuit. As a result,

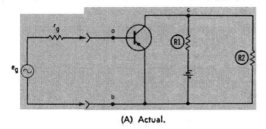

(A) Actual.

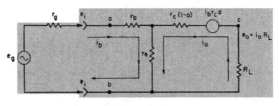

(B) Equivalent.

Fig. 4-9. Circuit of a common-emitter amplifier.

the r_b term of the equation is replaced by $r_b + R_b$, where R_b is the added resistance. In practice, the values of r_e and R_L are small relative to $r_c \, (1 - a)$ (r_c is in the range of 1 megohm). As a result, the values of r_e and R_L in the denominator can be eliminated.

$$R_i = r_b + \frac{r_e \, r_c}{r_c \, (1-a) + r_e + R_L} + \frac{r_e \, R_L}{r_c \, (1-a) \, r_e + R_L}$$

$$\approx r_b + \frac{r_e \, r_c}{r_c \, (1-a)} \text{, since } \frac{r_e \, R_L}{r_c \, (1-a)} \approx 0.$$

51

Now it can be seen that the factors affecting input resistance are r_b and $\dfrac{r_e}{1-a}$. A transistor with large common-base forward-current gain, a, will present a high input impedance. That is, a will be about 0.95 and $1-a$ will be very small (0.05). This will make the second term of the equation large, since $1-a$ is in the denominator. Additional emitter resistance can be added so that r_e is replaced with the term $r_e + R_E$ where R_E is the external series emitter resistance. This also increases the input resistance.

Finally, a resistance can be shunted across the input. The result is a parallel combination consisting of the shunt resistor and the input resistance. What factors affect the voltage gain? Here again the answer is in an equation.

$$A_v = \frac{R_L\,[r_c\,(1-a) - r_e]}{r_b\,[r_c\,(1-a) + r_e + R_L] + r_e\,(r_c + R_L)}$$

A number of factors can be removed from this equation when the relative magnitudes are considered. First, however, the equation must be put in a different form. Three terms are obtained when the terms in the numerator are multiplied.

$$A_v = \frac{(R_L)\,(r_c) - R_L\,(r_c)a - R_L\,r_e}{r_b\,[r_c\,(1-a) + r_e + R_L] + r_e\,(r_c + R_L)}$$

It is also necessary to multiply the terms in the denominator, and refactor.

$$A_v = \frac{(R_L)\,(r_c) - R_L\,(r_c)a - R_L\,r_e}{r_c\,[r_b\,(1-a) + r_e] + r_b\,r_e + r_b\,R_L + r_e\,R_L}$$

Three of the products in the denominator can be ignored because they are very small in relation to $r_c\,[r_b\,(1-a) + r_e]$. Thus:

$$A_v \approx \frac{R_L\,(r_c)}{r_c\,[r_b\,(1-a) + r_e]} - \frac{R_L\,(r_c)a}{r_c\,[r_b\,(1-a) + r_e]}$$
$$- \frac{R_L\,r_e}{r_c\,[r_b\,(1-a) + r_e]}$$

Since

$$\frac{R_L\,(r_c)}{r_c\,[r_b\,(1-a) + r_e]} - \frac{R_L\,r_e}{r_c\,[r_b\,(1-a) + r_e]} \approx 0$$

Then

$$A_v = \frac{-R_L\,(r_c)a}{r_c\,[r_b\,(1-a) + r_e]} = \frac{-R_L a}{r_b\,(1-a) + r_e}$$

52

It can now be more clearly seen that the load resistance, R_L, and the common-base current gain, a, are directly related to the voltage gain. In addition, it can be seen that the base resistance, r_b, and the emitter resistance, r_e, should be small.

Somewhat of a problem may be evident here. If the base and emitter resistances are made high (using external resistors) in order to provide high input resistance, the stage gain will be decreased. This is reasonable since the high input resistance will reduce the base current supplied from the input-voltage source. Design engineers faced with this problem often resort to a "trade-off." That is, they select compromise values of base and emitter resistance that will yield acceptable input resistance and yet provide reasonable gain.

Mathematically, it looks as if the "denominator" problem can be overcome by increasing the load-resistance term in the numerator. There are practical limitations, however. It will be recalled that the R_L term represents the parallel combination of the collector resistor and the input resistance of the following stage. If the collector-resistor value is increased, the combined resistance will still remain nearly the same. If the input resistance of the next stage is also increased, the gain of that stage will be reduced. Thus, the maximum gain of a stage is limited by the input resistance of the following stage.

The a term in the denominator is not much help. It can approach 1 if high-gain transistors are used but the $1 - a$ term in the numerator will not help at all since it is added to the r_e term. As can be seen, the component values shown in the schematics of this chapter represent compromise choices.

An electronic circuit can be represented as a voltage generator with an internal resistor in series with one of the output leads. This resistance is called the output resistance of the circuit. It is significant because it causes the output voltage to decrease as more current is drawn. It is desirable to keep the value of this resistance as low as possible. This reduces output voltage variations due to variations in the current drawn by the following circuit. What are the factors that affect output resistance? The complete story is that:

$$R_o = \frac{v_o}{i_o} = r_c \, (1 - a) + \frac{r_e \, (r_g + r_b + a\,r_c)}{r_g + r_b + r_e}$$

The term r_g represents the output resistance of the previous stage.

None of the terms can be ignored in this case. The value of r_c can be reduced if the transistor is biased to operate at fairly high quiescent current. The output resistance of the circuit can also be lowered if the output resistance of the preceding stage (r_g) is kept low. Typical values of output resistance range from 50 to 300 ohms.

Equations for the input resistance, output resistance, voltage gain, and current gain are derived from the loop-voltage equations describing the equivalent circuit. The loop voltage equations are:

$$e_i = (r_b + r_e) \, i_b + r_e \, i_o$$

$$0 = (r_e - r_c \, a) \, i_b + [r_c \, (1 - a) + r_e + R_L] \, i_o$$

The value of the loop currents are obtained by solving the simultaneous loop-voltage equations. They are:

$$i_b = \frac{e_i \, [r_e + r_c \, (1 - a) + R_L]}{r_b \, [r_e + r_c \, (1 - a) + R_L] + r_e \, (r_c + R_L)}$$

$$i_o = \frac{e_i \, (r_c \, a - r_e)}{r_b \, [r_e + r_c \, (1 - a) + R_L] + r_e \, (r_c + R_L)}$$

The loop-current equations are used to derive the equations for input resistance, voltage gain, current gain, and output resistance.

The above mentioned quantities are extremely important. The input resistance indicates the current that will be drawn by the circuit from the preceding stage. The voltage gain is important in both analysis and design work. This is also true of the current gain. The output resistance must be known because it affects the following stage. These quantities are easily derived using their basic definitions and the equations for the loop currents.

Input resistance, R_i, for a common-emitter is derived as follows:

$$R_i = \frac{e_i}{i_b} = \frac{e_i}{\dfrac{e_i \, [r_e + r_c \, (1 - a) + R_L]}{r_b \, [r_e + r_c \, (1 - a) + R_L] + r_e \, (r_c + R_L)}}$$

$$= \frac{r_b \, [r_e + r_c \, (1 - a) + R_L] + r_e \, (r_c + R_L)}{r_e + r_c \, (1 - a) + R_L}$$

$$= r_b + \frac{r_e \, (r_c + R_L)}{r_e + r_c \, (1 - a) + R_L}$$

The voltage gain, A_v, is derived as follows:

$$A_v = \frac{-e_o}{e_i} = \frac{-i_o \, R_L}{e_i}$$

54

$$= \frac{\left[\dfrac{-e_i(r_c a - r_e)}{r_b[r_e + r_c(1-a) + R_L] + r_e(r_c + R_L)} \right] R_L}{e_i}$$

$$= \frac{-(r_c a - r_e)R_L}{r_b[r_e + r_c(1-a) + R_L] + r_e(r_c + R_L)}$$

The current gain, A_i, is derived as follows:

$$A_i = \frac{i_o}{i_b} = \frac{\dfrac{e_i(r_c a - r_e)}{r_b[r_e + r_c(1-a) + R_L] + r_e(r_c + R_L)}}{\dfrac{e_i[r_e + r_c(1-a) + R_L]}{r_b[r_e + r_c(1-a) + R_L] + r_e(r_c + R_L)}}$$

$$= \frac{r_c a - r_e}{r_e + r_c(1-a) + R_L}$$

The output impedance of the common-emitter amplifier is derived using a slightly different equivalent circuit (Fig. 4-10).

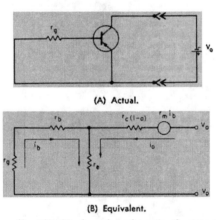

(A) Actual.

(B) Equivalent.

Fig. 4-10. Circuit used to determine the output resistance of a common-emitter amplifier.

This configuration results when a battery, representing the output voltage, is applied between the collector and emitter of the transistor. The ratio of output voltage to output current is considered to represent the value of an equivalent series-connected output resistance.

Note that the load resistance is disconnected from the circuit. This allows the rest of the transistor circuit to be treated as a generator which supplies current to the load resistance. Also note that a resistor is used to simulate the effect of the internal resistance in the input generator.

55

The voltage-loop equations for the new equivalent circuit are:

$$0 = (r_g + r_b + r_e)i_b + r_e i_o$$
$$e_o = (r_e - r_c a)i_b + [r_c (1 - a) + r_e]i_o$$

These simultaneous equations are solved to yield the output current.

$$i_o = \frac{e_o(r_g + r_b + r_e)}{[r_c (1 - a)](r_g + r_b + r_e) + r_e (r_g + r_b + ar_c)}$$

The output resistance, R_o, is then found to be:

$$R_o = \frac{e_o}{i_o} = \frac{e_o}{\dfrac{e_o(r_g + r_b + r_e)}{[r_c (1 - a)](r_g + r_b + r_e) + r_e (r_g + r_b + ar_c)}}$$

$$= \frac{r_c (1 - a)(r_g + r_b + r_e) + r_e (r_g + r_b + ar_c)}{r_g + r_b + r_e}$$

$$= r_c (1 - a) + \frac{r_e (r_g + r_b + ar_c)}{r_g + r_b + r_e}$$

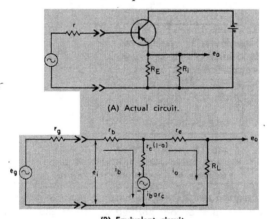

(A) Actual circuit.

(B) Equivalent circuit.

Fig. 4-11. A common-emitter amplifier.

Equivalent Circuit. The common-collector amplifier (Fig. 4-11) is often used as a resistance-changing stage. The common-collector amplifier (or emitter follower) presents a high input and low output resistance. The gain of an emitter follower, unfortunately, is always slightly less than 1.

56

The input resistance of an emitter follower is approximately:

$$R_1 \approx \frac{R_L}{1-a} \approx bR_L,$$

where $b = \dfrac{a}{1-a}$ and the term R_L represents the parallel combination of the emitter resistor and the input resistance of the following stage.

The output resistance of the emitter follower is approximately:

$$R_o \approx r_e + (r_b + r_g)(1-a)$$

$$R_o \approx r_e$$

The characteristics of a 2N525 transistor used in the three basic-circuit configurations is summarized in Fig. 4-12.

CIRCUIT CONFIGURATION		CHARACTERISTICS*	
COMMON EMITTER (CE)		moderate input impedance	(1.3 K)
		moderate output impedance	(50 K)
		high current gain	(35)
		high voltage gain	(—270)
		highest power gain	(40 db)
COMMON BASE (CB)		lowest input impedance	(35 Ω)
		highest output impedance	(1 M)
		low current gain	(—0.98)
		high voltage gain	(380)
		moderate power gain	(26 db)
COMMON COLLECTOR (CC) (EMITTER FOLLOWER)		highest input impedance	(350 K)
		lowest output impedance	(500 Ω)
		high current gain	(—36)
		unity voltage gain	(1.00)
		lowest power gain	(15 db)

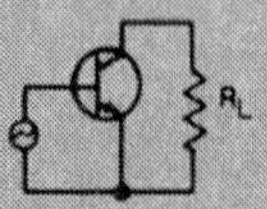

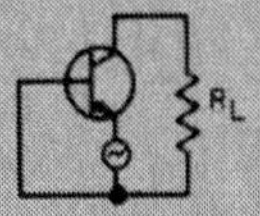

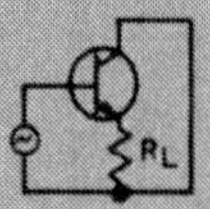

* Numerical values are typical for the 2N525 at audio frequencies with a bias of 5 volts and 1 ma., a load resistance of 10K, and a source (generator) resistance of 1K.

Reprinted, with permission, from the General Electric Transistor Manual, Fifth Edition

Fig. 4-12. Transistor circuit configurations.

TRANSISTOR PARAMETERS

The symbols r_c, r_e, r_b, and a have been used to represent the parameters of a transistor. There are, unfortunately, other systems of symbols used also. The one other most widely used is the H-parameters system. The relationship between the symbols (called the T equivalent-circuit parameters) used previously in this chapter and the H parameters is shown in Table 4-1.

TABLE 4-1.

Approximate Conversion Formulas

H Parameters and T Equivalent Circuit

(Numerical Values are Typical for the 2N525 at 1 ma, 5V)

Symbols		Common Emitter	Common Base	Common Collector	T Equivalent Circuit
IRE	Other				
h_{1e}	$h_{1e}, \dfrac{1}{Y_{11e}}$	1400 ohms	$\dfrac{h_{1b}}{1+h_{fb}}$	h_{1e}	$r_b + \dfrac{r_e}{1-\alpha}$
h_{re}	h_{12e}, μ_{be}	3.37×10^{-4}	$\dfrac{h_{1b} h_{ob}}{1+h_{fb}} - h_{rb}$	$1 - h_{re}$	$\dfrac{r_e}{(1-\alpha) r_c}$
h_{fe}, β	h_{21e}, β	44	$-\dfrac{h_{rb}}{1+h_{fb}}$	$-(1+h_{fe})$	$\dfrac{\alpha}{1-\alpha}$
h_{oe}	$h_{22e}, \dfrac{1}{Z_{22e}}$	27×10^{-6} mhos	$\dfrac{h_{ob}}{1+h_{fb}}$	h_{oe}	$\dfrac{1}{(1-\alpha) r_c}$
h_{1b}	$h_{11b}, \dfrac{1}{Y_{11}}$	$\dfrac{h_{1e}}{1+h_{fe}}$	31 ohms	$\dfrac{h_{1e}}{h_{fe}}$	$r_b + (1-\alpha) r_e$
h_{rb}	h_{12b}, μ_{ec}	$\dfrac{h_{1e} h_{oe}}{1+h_{fe}} - h_{re}$	5×10^{-4}	$h_{fe} - 1 - \dfrac{h_{1e} h_{oe}}{h_{fe}}$	$\dfrac{r_b}{r_c}$
h_{2b}, α	h_{21}, α	$-\dfrac{h_{fe}}{1+h_{fe}}$	-0.978	$-\dfrac{1+h_{rb}}{h_{rb}}$	$-\alpha$

h_{ob}	$h_{2z}, \frac{1}{Z_{zz}}$	$\frac{h_{oe}}{1+h_{fe}}$	0.60×10^{-6} mhos	$-\frac{h_{re}}{h_{fe}}$	$\frac{1}{r_c}$
h_{1c}	$h_{21c}, \frac{1}{Y_{11e}}$	h_{1e}	$\frac{h_{1b}}{1+h_{fb}}$	1400 ohms	$r_b + \frac{r_e}{1-a}$
h_{rc}	h_{12r}, μ_{be}	$1 - h_{re}$	1	1.00	$1 - \frac{r_e}{(1-a)r_c}$
h_{fc}	h_{21c}, α_{eb}	$-(1+h_{fe})$	$-\frac{1}{1+h_{fb}}$	-45	$-\frac{1}{1-a}$
h_{oc}	$h_{22r}, \frac{1}{Z_{22e}}$	h_{oe}	$\frac{h_{ob}}{1+h_{fb}}$	27×10^{-6} mhos	$\frac{1}{(1-a)r_c}$
a		$\frac{h_{fe}}{1+h_{fe}}$	$-h_{fb}$	$\frac{1+h_{fe}}{h_{fe}}$	0.978
r_c		$\frac{1+h_{fe}}{h_{oe}}$	$\frac{1-h_{rb}}{h_{ob}}$	$-\frac{h_{fe}}{h_{oe}}$	1.67 meg
r_e		$\frac{h_{re}}{h_{oe}}$	$h_{1b} - \frac{h_{rb}(1+h_{fb})}{h_{ob}}$	$\frac{1-h_{re}}{h_{oe}}$	12.5 ohms
r_b		$h_{1e} - \frac{h_{re}(1+h_{fe})}{h_{oe}}$	$\frac{h_{rb}}{h_{ob}}$	$h_{1e} + \frac{h_{fe}(1-h_{re})}{h_{oe}}$	840 ohms

Reprinted, with permission, from the General Electric Transistor Manual, Fifth Edition

Parameter Variations

In the discussion of equivalent circuits it was implied that parameters such as r_c, a, r_e, and r_b are constants. This is not completely true. They are constants only at one operating point on the characteristics curves. As long as the signal variations remain fairly small, the parameter values remain unchanged *at that operating point.* If the operating point of the circuit changes due to bias-voltage variations, temperature variations, or large signal variations, the values of the parameters will also change.

It is important to note that the electrical characteristics given in all transistor-data literature are obtained under a specified set of operating conditions. Other operating conditions will result in different electrical characteristics.

COMPLEMENTARY SYMMETRY IN DC AMPLIFIERS

The use of NPN and PNP transistors in similar circuits is called *complementary symmetry.* The circuits (Fig. 4-13) act like class-A push-pull amplifiers. Note the absence of the familiar paraphase device. This device is usually used to provide two identical signals, 180 degrees out-of-phase with each other. It is not required in this arrangement because each type of transistor responds differently to the input.

A positive-going base-voltage signal, for example, will cause greater collector-current flow in an NPN transistor. The same signal will cause reduced collector-current flow in a PNP. On the other hand, a negative-going signal will cause the reverse effect.

The transistors used in these circuits must have almost identical characteristics (the polarities of the currents and voltages will be opposite). As can be seen, a push-pull operation will result. The balanced output developed across points a and b is applied to the input resistance of the following stage.

Each transistor circuit often has identical resistive components. Biasing is obtained from a resistor connected between the base and the collector power supply. Additional biasing (and negative feedback) is obtained from an unbypassed emitter resistor. This circuit is used in the early stages of high-gain DC amplifiers. The main advantage of this circuit is that the temperature-dependent collector currents (I_{co}) of each transistor are cancelled when both flow through the load resistor. These currents flow in opposite directions in the NPN and the PNP transistors. Here again, it is important that the tempera-

60

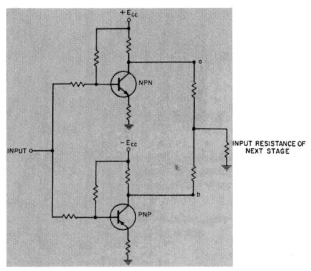

Fig. 4-13. A DC-amplifier stage using complimentary symmetry.

ture-dependent collector current of both transistors vary in an almost identical manner. In some cases, temperature-sensitive compensating networks may be used to correct for *minor* differences in this current.

REVIEW QUESTIONS

1. What are the causes of drift in transistor circuits?

2. Name a widely used drift-reduction circuit.

3. How does negative feedback extend the frequency response of an amplifier?

4. What are some of the operational considerations for any transistorized operational amplifier?

5. What resistances are represented by the load resistance in Fig. 4-9A?

6. How is the input resistance of a common-emitter amplifier increased?

7. What factors affect the voltage gain of a common-emitter amplifier?

8. How are equivalent circuit equations derived?

9. How is input resistance determined?

10. How is output resistance determined?

CHAPTER 5

Servo Amplifiers

Servo amplifiers are an essential part of any analog system that uses electric motors to provide physical motion.

Servo systems are used, among other things, to:

1. Drive indicating devices.
2. Drive conveyor belts at variable speeds.
3. Position automated machine tools.
4. Operate valves.
5. Rotate radar antennas.
6. Position missile-guidance devices.
7. Aim large guns.
8. Provide remote control for mechanical controls.

To fully appreciate the functioning of servo amplifiers, it is necessary to understand their function in the servo system (Fig. 5-1). The speed and the mechanical twisting force (torque) of AC and DC motors depends upon the magnitude of the voltage and current applied to the motor windings. The servo amplifier supplies these voltages and currents.

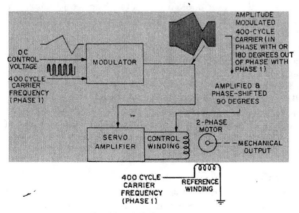

Fig. 5-1. A basic servo system.

The input to the servo amplifier is a small motor-control voltage often developed by analog-computing circuits. The servo amplifier amplifies this control voltage and puts it in a form suitable for driving the associated motor.

Two-phase AC motors are usually used to provide the desired mechanical motion. The DC control-voltages usually available are used to modulate a low-frequency AC "carrier" which actually drives the motor. The amplitude of this modulated carrier determines the speed and torque of the motor.

The two-phase motor has two separate windings energized by sine waves 90 degrees out-of-phase with each other. One winding (the reference winding) is continuously energized by an AC power source. The other winding (the control winding) is energized by the servo amplifier.

Motor rotation does not occur if the amplifier output is absent. As soon as the amplifier output voltage increases from zero, however, the motor begins to turn. The speed of the motor is proportional to the magnitude of this output voltage. The direction of rotation depends upon the phase of this output voltage in relation to the AC voltage applied to the reference winding of the motor. This phase is determined by the polarity of the DC control voltage applied to the modulator.

THE MODULATOR

The modulator (Fig. 5-2) is a diode ring-type often used for conventional AM modulation. The circuit shown was developed by N. F. Moody of the Canadian Defense Research Board and appears in the Handbook of Selected Semiconductor Circuits prepared for the U. S. Navy by Transistor Applications, Incorporated.

This ring modulator is best understood if some parts of the circuit is presented in an equivalent form (Fig. 5-3). The DC-input stage can be represented by a very low-value series resistor (a few hundred ohms) and a variable DC voltage.

In addition, the split secondary of transformer T1 can be considered as two AC generators having 70-volt peak voltages with respect to ground (point b). The output voltages of these equivalent generators (A and B) are always 180 degrees out-of-phase with respect to each other.

Basic Operation

The diode ring-modulator works by alternately causing a changing current to flow through one-half of the primary of transformer T2 and then through the other half at a 400-cycle

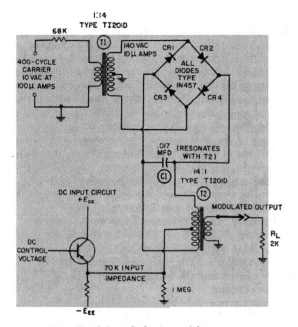

Fig. 5-2. A diode ring-modulator.

rate. Each half-cycle of changing carrier current produces a half-cycle of sinusoidal output voltage. The phase of this output voltage in relation to the 400-cycle carrier voltage depends upon the direction of current through each primary half.

Note that the DC control voltage is coupled to points d and e. Diodes CR1 and CR4 are forward biased when the DC control voltage is positive. This causes current flow from point d to point f and from point e to point f.

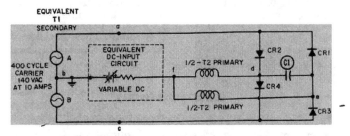

Fig. 5-3. Equivalent circuit of a diode ring-modulator.

65

Diodes CR2 and CR3 are forward biased when the DC control voltage is negative. In this case, the direction of current flow is reversed (from point f to points d and e).

Also note that when two of the diodes are forward biased by the DC control voltage, the other two are back-biased and cutoff. As long as the instantaneous amplitude of the carrier voltage is less than the DC control voltage, the cutoff diodes remain back biased and current flows through one of the conducting diodes and through one of the half-windings.

When one of the back-biased diodes becomes forward biased (the amplitude of carrier voltage exceeds the DC control voltage), the diode conducts and shorts point a to point b. This interrupts the current flowing through the half-winding. The result is that the output-voltage amplitude is clipped at the value it had when the current was interrupted.

The capacitor connected across the entire primary winding of transformer T2, however, filters the high-frequency components associated with the clipped half-cycle of sinewave so that a nearly sinusoidal output half-cycle occurs. The output has an amplitude approximately equal to the output voltage at the time of the clipping.

The capacitor operates by coupling the high-frequency components of the clipped voltage through the non-conducting half-winding. The high-frequency components are cancelled because they produce currents which flow in opposite directions in both halves of the center-tapped primary windings. That is, they produce magnetic fields which cancel each other.

The small short-circuit current produced in the secondary of transformer T1, when the diodes shorts points a and c together, is considerably below the maximum rated current of the transformer.

In this manner, the amplitude of each half-cycle of the 400-cycle carrier voltage is modulated by the DC control voltage. The polarity of the control voltage determines the phase of the modulated-carrier voltage output relative to the unmodulated-carrier voltage input. This is done as a result of the direction of current flow through the half-winding. This direction depends upon which diode is forward biased as a result of the polarity of the DC control voltage.

SERVO AMPLIFIERS

The servo amplifier consists of three functional circuit groups —the preamplifier, the driver, and the output stage. The preamplifier receives small modulated-carrier input currents and provides current gains of approximately 100. The driver receives the signals from the preamplifier, amplifies them, and provides two output signals 180 degrees out-of-phase with each other. This signal is required to drive the output stage which is usually a class-B power amplifier.

The Preamplifier

The preamplifier (Fig. 5-4) is a simple two-stage direct-coupled amplifier. Negative feedback is used to provide fairly stable gain for all of the frequency components of the 400-cycle modulated-carrier voltage.

Resistors R_E and R5 form a feedback voltage-divider which is energized by the emitter voltage of transistor X2. The DC

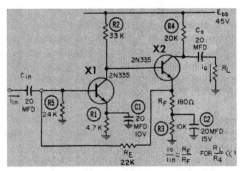

Fig. 5-4. 400-cycle preamplifier for operation
in temperatures from −55° to 125° C.

voltage developed across resistors R3 and R_F by the no-signal emitter current of transistor X2, causes a bias current to flow through the base circuit of transistor X1. The no-signal collector voltage of transistor X1 causes base bias current to flow in transistor X2.

The closed feedback loop between transistors X1 and X2 provides temperature and gain stability. This feedback loop compensates for variations in operating currents due to temperature variation. Any variation in operating currents are connected around the loop until they return to the element causing the variation. When they return to this element they are of opposite phase or polarity which considerably reduces the original variation.

Suppose, for example, the collector current of transistor X1 begins to increase due to a temperature rise. The following sequence of events will occur:

67

1. The collector voltage of transistor X1 begins to decrease because the increased collector current lowers the emitter-to-collector resistance of the transistor.
2. The decrease in collector voltage causes the base current of transistor X2 to be reduced.
3. The reduced base current of transistor X2 reduces the amount of collector current flowing through the emitter resistance.
4. The reduced emitter voltage of transistor X2 is coupled through the feedback resistors and causes the base current of transistor X1 to be reduced.
5. Thus the loop is closed. The reduced base current of transistor X1 reduces the collector current which started the voltage change circulating around the loop. At this point, the collector current is returned to the original value. Note that a tiny fraction of a volt change still exists. This change voltage is amplified as it passes through transistors X2 and X1 and causes the correction voltages and currents to be maintained. Because of the high gains around the feedback loop, the variations are reduced before they ever become too large.

When the modulated carrier is processed by the preamplifier a similar, but not identical, feedback loop exists. The capacitively-bypassed elements of the feedback loop, resistors R1 and R3, present a short circuit to signal voltages. As a result, a much smaller signal voltage is fed back from the emitter of transistor X2.

The bypassed emitter resistance of transistor X1 causes the signal input impedance to be quite small. The combined resistance of resistor R5 and the base input resistance of transistor X1 is approximately 100 ohms. If the modulator previously discussed were used, a series resistance of 1.9K would be required between the modulator output and the pre-amplifier input.

The details of the AC feedback loop are the same as those discussed in the negative feedback loop of the operational amplifier. In this case, however, the feedback current is 180 degrees out-of-phase with the input current.

Driver Circuit

The driver (Fig. 5-5) is a class-A push-pull amplifier using an output transformer with a center-tapped secondary winding in order to provide two output signals 180 degrees out-of-phase with each other. The output signals are taken from each end of the output transformer secondary and the center tap. Transis-

68

tor X3 drives the other two transistors which form the class-A push-pull amplifier. Resistors R3 and R_E form a feedback network that supplies DC bias current to the base of transistor X1 as well as supplying a small AC feedback.

An amplified version of the current drawn by the base of transistor X1 causes an emitter voltage at X1 which is coupled to the emitter of transistor X2. The DC base voltage of transistor X2 is held constant by a voltage-divider network which provides bias current.

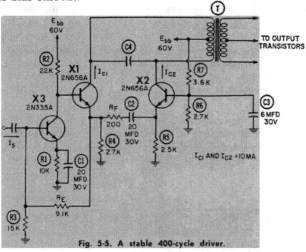

Fig. 5-5. A stable 400-cycle driver.

Bypass capacitor C3 keeps the base of transistor X2 at an AC ground potential. Consequently, the signal variations at the emitter of transistor X2 results in a base-to-emitter voltage 180 degrees out-of-phase with the input current to transistor X1. That is, the voltage at both emitters is in phase with the input signal current. However, the base-to-emitter voltage of transistor X2 is equal to the zero voltage (for AC) at the base of X2 *minus* the signal voltage at the emitter. This results in a base-to-emitter voltage 180 degrees out-of-phase (the minus sign) with the base-to-emitter voltage of transistor X1. This arrangement is very similar to the familiar grounded-grid amplifier or the cathode coupling used in multivibrators.

The out-of-phase base-to-emitter currents cause the transistor collector currents to be 180 degrees out-of-phase with respect to each other. As a result, the simultaneous and changing collector currents flowing through the center-tapped transformer primary create magnetic fields which add together to

69

produce almost twice the output voltage that can be produced by a single stage. The term "push-pull" itself suggest two forces moving an object. If one force is pushing and the other force is pulling, the forces acting on the object will be the sum of both.

Any transformer has capacitance between turns of the insulated wire used for the windings. The resonant frequency of the combined inductance and winding capacitance may be within the range of the component frequencies of the modulated carrier. In this case, the transformer would oscillate (until it is damped out) when activated by the resonant-frequency component. Capacitor C4, however, tunes the transformer to a resonant frequency of 400 cycles. As a result, the transformer oscillates at the carrier frequency and does not over-emphasize any other frequency components.

Output Stage

The servo power-output stage (Fig. 5-6) provides the power for the control winding of the two-phase motor. Each power transistor conducts on alternate half-cycles. As a result, the total current flowing through the control winding is a sine

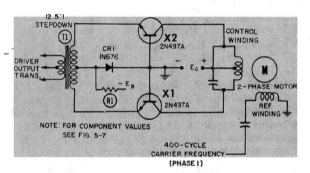

Fig. 5-6. A servo power-output stage.

wave. One-half cycle of the sine wave is supplied by one power transistor and the other half is supplied by the second transistor.

Power supply E_B and resistor R1 supply a small bias current to the transistors. The bias current keeps them slightly above cutoff, and as a result, variations in the current required to bring them out of cutoff do not cause distortions of the transformer current. That is, the bias current allows heavy conduc-

70

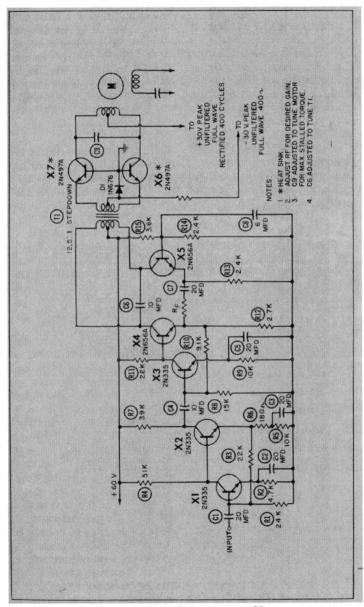

Fig. 5-7. A 2-watt, 400-cycle servo amplifier.

71

tion without any delay following the application of a half-cycle of voltage. This means that conduction current is not delayed because of the transistor having to first be brought out of cutoff.

The diode prevents reverse currents through the base-emitter junctions of the transistors when reverse voltage is applied by the input transformer. Capacitor C tunes the motor winding to be resonant at 400 cycles. This prevents the unwanted oscillations discussed earlier.

The Complete Servo Amplifier

The complete servo amplifier (Fig. 5-7) merely consists of the circuits just discussed. Note that the preamplifier is capacitively coupled to the driver stage and that the driver and output stages are inductively coupled. The output stage is coupled inductively, or more accurately, magnetically to the motor's rotor.

REVIEW QUESTIONS

1. What are some applications of servo systems?

2. What determines the speed and torque of a motor?

3. What causes a two-phase motor to rotate?

4. What are the functional parts of a servo amplifier?

5. What is the function of the preamplifier?

6. What is the function of the driver?

7. What is the function of the output stage?

8. How is temperature and gain stability achieved in the preamplifier?

9. How does the driver create a paraphase output?

10. Why are transformers tuned at the power-line frequencies?

CHAPTER 6

Digital Computers

This portion of the book is devoted to explaining how the various digital computer functions are accomplished by transistorized circuits.

LOGIC FUNCTIONS

There are four basic functions performed in the digital computer: (1) the AND function, (2) the OR function, (3) the negation (inversion) function, and (4) the temporary-storage function (flip-flop). Each of these is performed by a specific logic circuit. As mentioned before, thousands of these circuit types are used in the digital computer.

Signal Voltages

In a digital computer, only two signal conditions are usually used. These conditions, represented either by voltage levels or by pulses, correspond to yes-no, true-false, present-absent, logical 1-logical 0, or on-off.

All digital computer circuits respond to these signals. A pulse or a voltage level that operates a circuit represents the yes, true, present, logical 1, or on condition. These voltage levels range from fractions of a volt to about 10 volts, with a polarity either positive or negative. A ground signal, which turns off both NPN and PNP transistors, is usually used to represent the no, false, absent, logical 0, or off condition. In some cases the "no" signal is the opposite polarity of the "yes" signal.

In control applications, the yes-no indications represent the condition of the process being controlled. These yes-no signals represent the answers to such questions as: Is the power on? Is the temperature above 90 degrees Fahrenheit? Are we ready for the next process?

In data processing and arithmetic operations, the yes-no signals represent the digits of a number. The binary-number sys-

tem makes it possible to represent any number as a series of
1's and 0's. The "yes" signal-condition corresponds to the 1's
in a binary number and the "no" signal-condition represents
the 0's.

The AND Circuit

The AND circuit is a configuration providing a yes (or logical 1) output *when EACH input signal* is logical 1.

The OR Circuit ·

The OR circuit is a configuration providing a logical 1 *when
ANY input signal* is logical 1.

The Inverter Circuit

The inverter circuit reverses any input signal. That is, if a
logical 1 is applied to an inverter input, a logical 0 appears at
the output. On the other hand, if a logical 0 is applied to the
inverter input, a logical 1 appears at the output. It will be
shown that this seemingly odd function is quite useful.

The Flip-Flop

The flip-flop is an electronic toggle switch which an electrical
pulse applied to the "set" input turns on. The output then supplies a gate voltage until the flip-flop is turned off by another
pulse applied to the "reset" input. This type of circuit is often
used as a means of storing a logical 1 until it is needed at a
later time. Practically every circuit configuration found in any
digital computer will consist of combinations of these four basic
circuits.

TIMING AND FREQUENCY DIVISION

Every operation in digital computers is synchronized by timing clock-pulses. These clock pulses are used as AND circuit
inputs. As a result, the AND circuits will not operate until the
clock pulse is applied.

Clock-Pulse Generation

Clock pulses are continuously generated at very precise intervals, usually by a frequency-stable sine-wave oscillator (Fig.
6-1). The sine waves are then used to synchronize pulse generators (blocking oscillators). The width of the clock pulses produced by this method usually range from about 1/10 of a microsecond ($\frac{1}{10,000,000}$ of a second) to 1/2 microsecond with the

interval between them about one microsecond. An oscillator frequency of one megacycle is used to produce such pulses and is referred to as a *one-megacycle clock.*

Frequency Division. The clock pulses are the primary computer-time reference. Situations do occur, however, in which it is desired to operate at lower repetition rates. This is done by a count-down or frequency-division arrangement (Fig. 6-2).

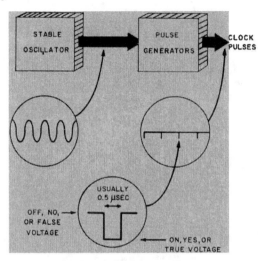

Fig. 6-1. Clock-pulse generation.

In the earlier discussion of the flip-flop it was noted that a pulse applied to the "set" input would turn on the output gate-voltage. It was also noted that another pulse applied to the "reset" input would turn it off.

Another way of operating a flip-flop consists of connecting the "set" and "reset" inputs together and is called *complementing* or *toggling.* In this arrangement, each pulse applied to the flip-flop changes the state. That is, if the flip-flop is on (set), the next pulse turns it off (resets). The next applied pulse turns it on again (sets), and so on. As a result, *one gate voltage is generated for every two input pulses applied* (Fig. 6-2). This process represents a division by two. That is, one gate occurs for every two clock pulses applied.

Note that this gate voltage is applied to an AND circuit. The other input to the AND circuit is the same clock pulses used to operate the flip-flop. Consequently, the gate voltage

75

occurs in coincidence with only every other clock pulse. Thus, the AND circuit responds to every other clock pulse only. This results in a series of timing pulses at the AND-circuit output, which occur at half the repetition frequency of the clock pulses originally applied. When division by four is desired, two frequency dividers are connected together. Division by eight occurs when three frequency dividers are connected together, and so on.

TRANSISTORS AS SWITCHES

In digital applications the transistor is used as a two-position switch. There is a very low resistance between the emitter and collector when the transistor switch is closed, and a very high resistance when it is open. Special switching transistors are

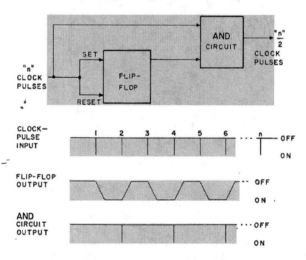

Fig. 6-2. Frequency division.

used for this purpose. The transistor switch is opened and closed by current flowing between the base and the emitter.

A typical transistor switch is shown in Fig. 6-3. The closure of the mechanical switch in the base circuit causes emitter-to-base current to flow. As a result, the emitter-to-collector resistance becomes very low and the collector voltage goes from —25 volts (the yes condition) to approximately zero volts (the no condition). When the base switch is opened, the base current is interrupted and the collector voltage returns to —25 volts.

The value of collector load-resistance provides a load line which causes the circuit operation to extend from transistor cutoff (small collector current, high resistance) to transistor saturation (maximum collector current, low resistance).

The resistance in series with the base determines the amount of base-current flow. That is, the base resistor forms a series circuit from the base battery through the base-emitter resistance of the transistor and back to the grounded battery terminal. The base-emitter resistance is fairly small, and so the amount of base current is often determined primarily by the value of the series resistor.

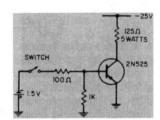

Fig. 6-3. A basic transistor switch.

The resistance connected between the base and ground reduces collector leakage-current when the base switch is open. This leakage current occurs at the junction of the transistor due to moisture or impurities in the semiconductor material. The resistor, which has a very low value compared to the open-circuit base-emitter resistance, bypasses the leakage current which would otherwise flow across the base-emitter junction of the transistor and cause an undesirable output voltage. However, during conditions of heavy base-emitter current flow (saturation), the low emitter-base resistance shorts the external resistor. This condition is not undesirable at this time since the leakage current is small and is only significant during the transistor cutoff condition.

Design Considerations

The load lines for transistor switches are constructed in the same manner as the load lines for vacuum-tube amplifiers. The value of maximum collector voltage and saturation current is obtained from the engineering data and collector characteristics provided by the manufacturer. The correct value of load resistor R_L is:

$$R_L = \frac{V_{CE} \text{ (Max)}}{I_C \text{ (Saturation)}}$$

77

The value of base current which flows from emitter to base is controlled by the base-to-switch resistor. The numerical value of base current I_B which will be required to cause saturation is determined from the equation:

$$I_B \approx \frac{I_c \text{ (Saturation)}}{\text{Transistor DC Current Gain } (H_{fe})}$$

The values of H_{FE} for the transistor being used can be obtained from the $H_{FE} - I_c$ curves supplied by the manufacturer.

The desired value of base current is obtained using the following equation:

$$I_B = \frac{E_{bb}}{R_s + R_E}$$

where R_s is the series resistor and R_E is the internal ohmic resistance between the transistor emitter and base. The value of R_E in germanium transistors is in the order of 20 to 50 ohms during heavy conduction.

Finally, consideration must be given to loading problems. A load resistor connected from collector to ground will create a voltage divider (with the collector resistor) when the transistor is cutoff. Thus, it must be remembered that the output voltage will not be the supply voltage but will be some smaller value determined by the relative values of load and collector-load resistance.

TRANSISTOR TRANSIENT RESPONSE

In digital computers it is often necessary to switch states in a few tenths of a microsecond. Consequently, the question of transient response becomes quite important.

Capacitive Effects

Unfortunately, there is capacitance at both the collector-base and emitter-base junctions. As a result, it is necessary to deal with exponential-voltage rises and decays, and charging and discharging currents.

Example of Capacitive Effects. An example of the problems introduced by capacitance is shown in Fig. 6-4. When the switch in the base circuit is closed (leading edge of waveform *b*):

1. Current flows from the base to the +10-volt supply (waveform *d*). Note that the diagram shows conventional current flow (i.e. opposite direction to electron flow). The initial current flow, however, represents a discharge of the

emitter-to-base capacitance. All of this stored charge, which is not composed of collector-current carriers, must be discharged before current can actually flow *through* the emitter-to-base junction and thus provide carriers for the collector current.

2. After a delay time, t_d, the collector current begins to flow. As a result, the collector voltage begins to decrease (waveform *e*).

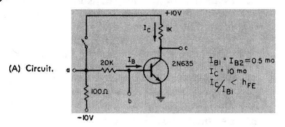

(A) Circuit.

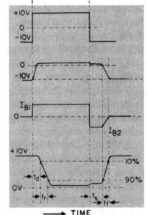

(B) Waveform generated at "a" by switch.

(C) Waveform at "b" showing forward bias on base during saturation.

(D) Base-current waveform. Note reverse current I_{B2} due to base bias during saturation.

(E) Collector waveform showing standard notation of response times.

Fig. 6-4. Transistor transient response.

3. The collector current increases exponentially until it reaches the desired value. The collector voltage, of course, *decreases* in the same manner.

4. At this point, the circuit has reached its steady-state value. As long as the switch remains closed, the waveforms remain constant.

When the switch is opened again (trailing edge of waveform *b*):

1. The voltage at point *A*, in Fig. 6-4A, becomes −10 volts (waveform *b*). However, since there are still collector-current carriers in the base-collector region, collector current continues to flow until all of the collector-current carriers are drawn out of the base region. This condition is called *carrier storage* and the time required to draw them out is called *storage time*, t_s. Note that the direction of base-current flow reverses as these carriers are drawn out. Also note, that the base voltage and the collector voltage changes very little in this interval.
2. When the stored carriers are completely drawn out, the transistor begins to cut off. This effect is shown in the interval of *fall time*, t_f. As can be seen, the base current decreases to zero, the collector current also decreases to zero, the collector voltage rises to the cutoff value, and the emitter-base junction is charged to −10 volts.

Reduction of Transient Response Time

There are many procedures used to reduce the various delays that have been discussed.

Delay time is reduced by using low-amplitude base-cutoff voltages in order to decrease the initial emitter-base charge. In addition, the value of the series base-resistor (base drive-resistor) is reduced. This reduces the charging time-constant. Delay time becomes negligible when high emitter-base current allows rapid discharge of the input capacitance.

Rise time is considerably reduced by a process called overdriving. This consists of using a base-current pulse providing two or three times the base current required for driving the transistor into the saturation region. Overdriving can *reduce* the rise time by a factor of 6. Note that overdriving also helps to reduce delay time.

Storage time is reduced by the method shown in the example, by actually reversing the polarity of the base drive-voltage (Fig. 6-4B). This draws the collector-current carriers out of the base region as fast as possible.

Another method used to reduce storage time is to prevent the transistor from going into the saturation region. This limits the number of collector-current carriers in the base region. The subject of saturation and non-saturation is discussed later.

Fall time is reduced using the same overdrive technique used to reduce rise time. The same reverse base drive-voltage used to reduce storage time also reduces the fall time.

Compensating Networks. The input circuit of a switching transistor can be represented by an equivalent circuit consist-

80

ing of a resistor shunted by a capacitor. A compensation network to improve response time can be used (Fig. 6-5). This provides a capacitive voltage-divider which will respond to the *changes* in the input voltage.

EFFECT OF TEMPERATURE ON DIGITAL CIRCUITS

The temperature of transistor junctions affect circuit operation. In some cases, variations due to increased temperature can result in undesirable operation of cascaded stages or can even result in destruction of a transistor.

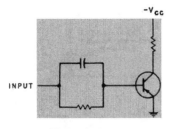
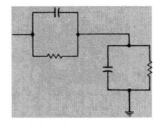

(A) Actual circuit.   (B) Equivalent circuit.

Fig. 6-5. A compensating network to improve response time.

Temperature and Cutoff Current

Even when the emitter-base junction is back biased, a small current flows. The magnitude of this current, called the cutoff current (I_{co}), is a function of temperature. That is, it increases as junction temperature rises. This base current, in turn, causes a collector current to flow which has a magnitude equal to the current gain times I_{co}.

The Effect of I_{co}. The effect of this undesirable collector current caused by I_{co} is twofold. First, the heat generated by it tends to increase I_{co} which, in turn, causes higher collector current. This process of positive feedback, called *thermal runaway,* can increase until it destroys the transistor due to the temperatures generated by the ever-increasing collector current.

The second effect is that of creating a false signal. The collector-current change affects the base current of the following stage, and so on, until a false signal is created along the chain.

Reducing Temperature Effects

The most direct method of reducing the effect of I_{co} (Fig. 6-6) consists of using a bias supply and resistor to remove the col-

81

lector-current carriers generated as a result of temperature (I_{co}). The values of V_{TC} and R_{TC} are selected so that

$$\frac{V_{TC}}{R_{TC}} = I_{co}.$$

The resistance R_{TC}, however, rarely varies with temperature in the same way as I_{co}. Thus, this method is limited in situations with a wide range of ambient temperatures. Another approach is used in such cases (Fig. 6-7). Here, a diode is used in place of R_{TC} and is selected to have a reverse current that varies with temperature in the same manner as I_{co}.

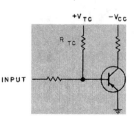

Fig. 6-6. Resistive temperature-compensation to reduce I_{co}.

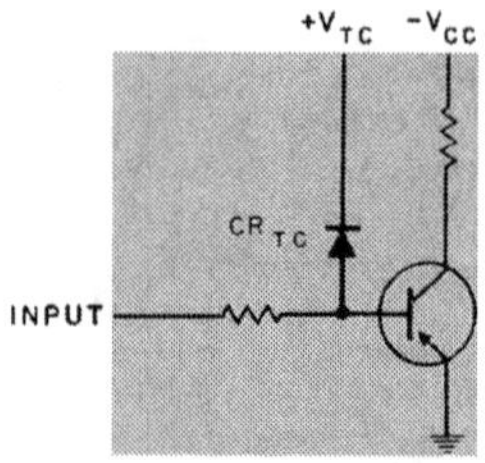

Fig. 6-7. Semiconductor temperature-compensation to reduce I_{co}.

SATURATED AND NON-SATURATED CIRCUITS

The saturation region of transistor operation is defined as the condition in which both junctions of a transistor are forward biased. That is, when the emitter-base junction is forward biased and I_B and I_c are very large, the voltage developed across the ohmic resistance of the emitter and base is very high. As a result, the base portion of the collector-base junction becomes negative with respect to the collector portion. This also forward biases the collector-base junction.

This condition can be visualized with the aid of an equivalent circuit (Fig. 6-8) in which the two junctions of the transistor are shown as being similar to separate diodes. The collector-base junction has a back resistance that is a function of base current I_B. To illustrate this relationship, a current generator is shown connected across the equivalent collector-base diode. Thus, the voltage at the base portion of the collector-base junction (equivalent diode cathode) can become more negative than the collector portion of the junction (diode plate).

Saturation is represented in the common emitter-collector characteristics (Fig. 6-9) as the area to the left of the nearly-vertical line which drops to a collector voltage of zero.

82

Saturated Circuits

Circuits driven into the saturation region of the transistor operating characteristics are popular because of their simplicity (Fig. 6-10). In addition, fewer components are required and the saturation collector-voltages are small and stable.

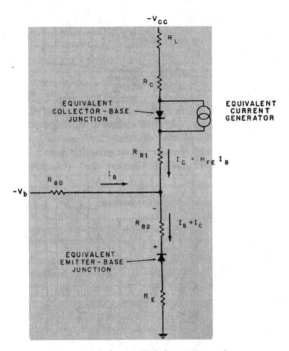

Fig. 6-8. Equivalent circuit of a PNP transistor.

The saturated circuit, as previously mentioned, has a large stored-charge in the base region. This results in a definite time required to draw out this charge before the transistor can be turned off. This limits the circuit response time. In addition, a reverse voltage must be used to reduce this storage time. This requires a high trigger power from the preceding stage. Non-saturated circuits are used to overcome these limitations.

Non-Saturated Circuits

Non-saturated circuits have devices which limit collector or base current.

83

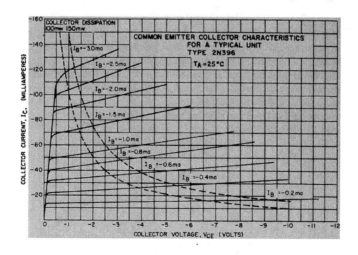

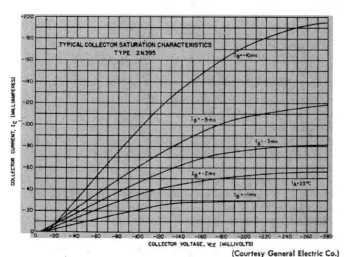

(Courtesy General Electric Co.)

Fig. 6-9. Typical transistor characteristic curves.

Collector-Voltage Clamping. The simplest way to limit this current is to connect a diode to the collector (Fig. 6-11) in such a way as to clamp the collector voltage above the saturation value. This prevents saturation because it does not allow the collector-base junction to become forward biased. That is, the diode conducts when the collector voltage rises from the nega-

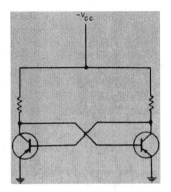

Fig. 6-10. A saturated flip-flop circuit.

tive supply-voltage to a fixed level a few volts below the saturation value (more negative than the saturation voltage).

The conducting diode connects a negative voltage, —E, to the collector. Since this negative voltage (diode supply) does not vary appreciably with current loading, the collector voltage re-

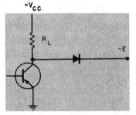

Fig. 6-11. Clamping the collector voltage to prevent saturation.

mains at —E volts. When NPN transistors are used, the polarity of the supply voltages and the diode connection are reversed.

Collector-Current Clamping. A more efficient method of preventing saturation (Fig. 6-12) consists of using the collector voltage to operate a diode which bypasses any base current that might rise above the level of saturation.

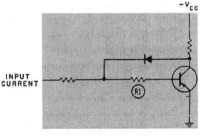

Fig. 6-12. Clamping the collector current to prevent saturation.

85

When the overdrive base-current has caused the collector voltage to approach the saturation value, the diode becomes forward biased and diverts the base current from the transistor into the collector load-circuit. This current is small compared to the collector current, and therefore has little effect on the load circuit. The value of R_1 is chosen so that its voltage drop is a fraction of a volt greater than the desired value of collector voltage. This voltage drop is developed by the base current.

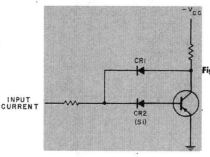

Fig. 6-13. Another method of clamping to prevent saturation.

Unfortunately, variations in base drive-current, current gain, or in resistance values will alter the collector clamp-voltage. This occurs because the collector will be clamped to the voltage developed across R_1.

The collector clamp-voltage is less sensitive to variations when a silicon diode replaces R_1 (Fig. 6-13). This type of diode maintains a constant voltage for a considerable range of currents and thus stabilizes the collector at a value of approximately 0.7 volts (the constant drop across the silicon diode).

REVIEW QUESTIONS

1. What are the four basic functions performed in a digital computer?
2. What are the two digital computer signal conditions?
3. What do the two signal conditions represent?
4. What does an AND circuit do?
5. What does an OR circuit do?
6. What does an inverter circuit do?
7. What does a flip-flop do?
8. What are clock pulses and for what are they used?
9. How does a transistor act as a switch?
10. What are some of the transient factors affecting transistor response?

CHAPTER 7

Logic Circuits

The conditions causing a computer circuit response are often represented symbolically using Boolean-algebra notations. The symbols of Boolean algebra and their meaning are as follows:

A, B, C, etc.   Signal inputs or specific conditions.

A+B   Signal A *or* signal B *or* both will operate the circuit (cause a "yes" output).

AB   The circuit will operate only when signal A *and* B are simultaneously present.

$\overline{A}$ A "yes" output will occur when the "A" signal is *not* present (a "no" input).

$\overline{AB}$ A "yes" output will occur when both signals are *not* present ("no" inputs). A "no" output will occur when *both* signals *are* present.

$\overline{A+B}$ A "yes" output will occur when both signals are *not* present. A "no" output will occur if either (A *or* B) signal is present.

COMMON LOGIC SYSTEMS

There are six systems of logic commonly used. They are:
1. Resistor-Transistor Logic, RTL.
2. Resistor-Capacitor-Transistor Logic, RCTL.
3. Direct-Coupled Transistor Logic, DCTL.
4. Diode Logic, DL.
5. Low-Level Logic, LLL.
6. Current-Mode Logic, CML.

Resistor-Transistor Logic (RTL)

This logic system uses one basic circuit consisting of resistors and transistors. These circuits can be connected together in

87

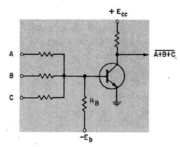

Fig. 7-1. A transistorized
NOR circuit.

ways which cause them to provide the AND, OR, storage, and inversion functions.

The basic circuit is called a NOR circuit which is short for Negated (inverted) OR circuit (Fig. 7-1). The transistor of this circuit will remain cutoff as long as all inputs are at ground potential (*off* condition). If any input goes to the *on* condition, base current flows and the transistor conducts and becomes saturated. Resistor R_B provides temperature stability.

Since the transistor shown is an NPN, the *yes* input voltage must be positive in order to cause circuit operation. This means that a *cutoff* transistor provides a *yes* output voltage at the collector. It can now be seen where the inversion comes into play. The single transistor inverts the base voltage when the output is taken at the collector. Thus, if any input is *yes*, the output goes to *no*. This is an inverted OR function.

Suppose a normal OR function is desired. To obtain it, merely invert the NOR-circuit output. This is done by connecting the output of the first NOR circuit to one of the inputs of a second NOR circuit (Fig. 7-2). The other inputs to the second NOR circuit are not used. As a result of this arrangement, if any input to the first circuit becomes *yes*, it's output becomes *no*.

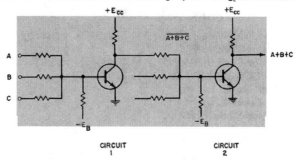

Fig. 7-2. NOR circuits performing the OR function.

The *no* output of the first NOR circuit causes the second NOR circuit to provide a *yes* output.

When the operation of the two NOR circuits are combined, the OR-function response results. That is, a *yes* voltage at any one of the three inputs to the first NOR circuit results in a *yes* voltage at the output of the second NOR circuit.

From a circuit point of view, when a *yes* input (positive voltage) is applied to the first transistor it conducts and its collector voltage approaches zero. The low collector voltage is applied to the base of the second transistor, and since this low base-input voltage does not cause significant base-current flow, the second transistor is cutoff. Under these conditions, a relatively high voltage (*yes* indication) appears at the collector of the second transistor.

Resistor-Capacitor-Transistor Logic (RCTL)

This logic system is the same as RTL except that capacitors are used to increase switching speed (Fig. 7-3). These capacitors can be thought of as part of a compensating network. Looking at it another way, when the capacitors are charging and

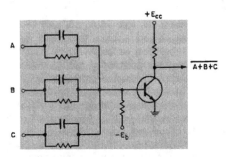

Fig. 7-3. A resistor-capacitor-transistor logic (RCTL) circuit is very similar to a resistor-transistor logic circuit.

discharging, they bypass the base drive resistors and provide a peak drive current. This peak drive current increases transistor-switching speed.

Direct-Coupled Transistor Logic (DCTL)

The DCTL system uses small signal levels which drive the transistors directly. The internal resistance of the driving-current source limits the maximum drawn.

A DCTL AND circuit (Fig. 7-4A) consists of two series transistors and provides a *yes* output (positive voltage) when both

89

inputs are *no* (zero volts). This occurs because both series transistors are cut off and most of the voltage drop in the circuit occurs across them. Logically, this condition indicates that signals at A and B are not *yes*.

When input A goes positive and input B remains at ground, the high resistance of the cutoff series transistor associated with input B prevents appreciable base-current flow in the other transistor. This, in turn, prevents an increase in its collector current, and consequently, the circuit output remains nearly constant at the positive value.

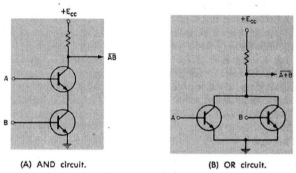

(A) AND circuit.   (B) OR circuit.

Fig. 7-4. Direct-coupled transistor logic (DCTL) circuits.

If input B goes positive and input A remains at ground, the high resistance of the A transistor prevents appreciable collector-current flow in the other. As in the case above, the output voltage remains at the positive value.

When both inputs become positive, however, both series transistors conduct heavily and the output voltage becomes close to zero volts. Logically, this condition indicates that A and B are *yes*.

Note that a *no* output results when both inputs are *yes*. This is called *negative logic* in that a logical function and an inversion are performed by each circuit. As in the case of the NOR circuit, a second stage of inversion is required to provide a *yes* output when both inputs are *yes*.

A DCTL OR circuit (Fig. 7-4B) consists of two transistors in parallel. When both inputs are at ground, the output is at a positive voltage. Logically this means A or B are not *yes*. However, if either input becomes positive, the associated transistor conducts and brings the output voltage to near zero. Thus, the circuit indicates that one of the inputs $(A$ or $B)$ is *yes*. Here again, a *no* output results when one of the inputs becomes *yes*.

90

Diode Logic (DL)

The DL system uses diodes to perform logical functions. A DL circuit consists of two or more diodes connected to a load resistor and used as voltage sensitive switches.

An OR circuit designed to work with positive (*yes*) signals (Fig. 7-5A) has all of the diode cathodes connected to one end of the load resistor with a negative voltage supply connected to the other. When all inputs are more negative than the supply voltage (*no* condition) the diodes are all cut off (switch open) because their plates are more negative than their cathodes. As a result, the output voltage is nearly equal to the negative supply voltage. This represents a *no* condition. Thus, the output of the DL OR circuit is *no* when each input is *no*.

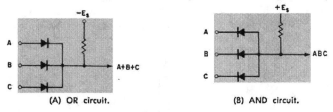

| (A) OR circuit. | (B) AND circuit. |

Fig. 7-5. Diode logic (DL) circuits.

However, if *any* input becomes positive (*yes* condition), the associated diode becomes forward biased and conducts heavily (switch closed). The current flowing in the circuit develops a positive output voltage. The value of this voltage is nearly equal to the input voltage. That is, the output voltage is equal to the input voltage minus the small voltage drop across the diode. Thus, any *yes* input will cause a *yes* output.

An AND circuit designed to work with positive (*yes*) signals (Fig. 7-5B) has all diode plates connected to a common load resistor which, in turn, is connected to a positive voltage supply. In this arrangement all of the diodes conduct when all of the inputs are negative (*no* condition). The output voltage during this time is also negative. That is, the input voltages are connected through the diodes to the output, except for the small voltage drop across the diodes.

When any one of the inputs become positive, the negative voltage connected through the other diodes causes the diode associated with the positive input to be cut off. The output of the circuit, however, remains negative until all of the diodes are cut off by positive voltages connected to the cathodes. When all inputs are positive, all of the diodes are cut off and the out-

91

put voltage is almost equal to the positive supply voltage. Thus, the circuit provides a *yes* output when all inputs are *yes*.

In both the OR and the AND circuit, the diodes may never be completely cut off. However, the current flows are small (high diode resistance) compared to the heavy-conduction current (low diode resistance). This means the output voltage will still be very close to the power-supply voltage.

Low-Level Logic (LLL)

In the LLL system a diode logic-circuit is used to drive an inverting amplifier. Small signal-voltage variations are used so that the transistors are not saturated. The negative output from the DL OR circuit (Fig. 7-6) causes the diode to conduct heavily. The resulting negative voltage at the diode plate cuts off the transistor, making the circuit output positive when all inputs are negative.

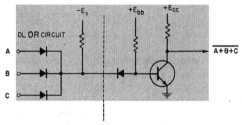

Fig. 7-6. A low-level logic (LLL) circuit.

If any of the circuit inputs become positive, the diode will be cutoff because the cathode becomes more positive than the plate. The positive supply voltage then causes the transistor to conduct, with the result that the output voltage drops to a lower value. As can be seen, this is an inverted OR-function. When all inputs are *no*, the output is *yes*. When *any* input is *yes*, the output becomes *no*.

Low-level logic uses low signal-voltage variations. This prevents transistor saturation and thus decreases switching time.

Current-Mode Logic (CML)

Current-mode logic circuits (Fig. 7-7) look somewhat like direct-coupled transistor logic circuits and work much the same way. There is one major difference, however. CML does not use saturated transistors. Saturation is prevented by the common-emitter resistance which limits base-current flow. In addition, the emitter resistor provides a non-inverted output. This occurs

92

because the collector current, which develops the output voltage, is only present when the logic conditions are *yes*.

The common-base current amplifier at the right of the circuit is similar to a ground-grid vacuum-tube amplifier—it does not invert the input signal applied between the emitter and the base. The common-base configuration used in this stage provides high-current outputs without excessively loading the logic circuit. A summary of the various types of logic systems is shown in Fig. 7-8.

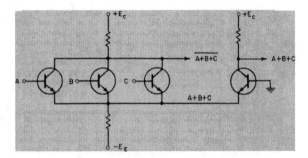

Fig. 7-7. A current-mode logic (CML) circuit.

INVERSION AND INTERCHANGABILITY OF *AND* AND *OR* FUNCTIONS

In the discussion of the types of logic it was noted that most transistorized logic circuits introduce a polarity inversion when they perform the basic AND or OR logic function. For example, it was seen that inputs that should produce an OR output actually produce a *not* OR output (NOR).

In the earlier discussion it was shown how a second stage of inversion could be added to a NOR circuit to provide an OR output. Many digital computers, however, make use of the inverted or negative functions. In fact, as will be seen, negative-OR circuits can be used to perform the AND function! The use of negative functions is possible because of the relationship between signals and their inverted form.

Relationship of Signals and Their Inverted Form

Take the case of a signal called A. It can only have one of two possible values. Suppose A is *no*, *off*, logical *0*, or *absent*. This will mean that the voltage representing A will be zero. Situations often arise in digital computers in which a circuit is needed that will operate when a condition, represented by

93

NAME	TYPICAL CIRCUIT (Positive signals are defined as 1)
RTL Resistor transistor logic (NOR)	
RCTL Resistor capacitor transistor logic	
DCTL Direct coupled transistor logic	
DL Diode logic	
LLL Low level logic	
CML Current mode logic	

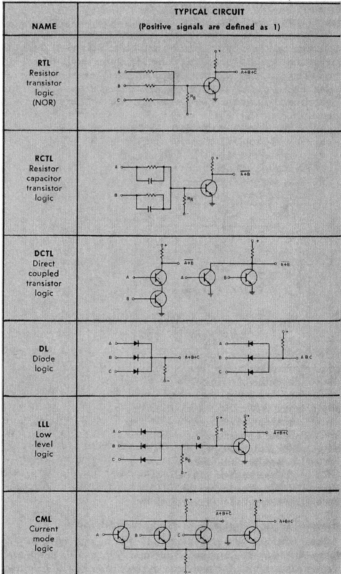

Reprinted, with permission, from the General Electric Transistor Manual, Fifth Edition

Fig. 7-8.

94

DESCRIPTION	FEATURES	SUITABLE TRANSISTORS	
		Germanium	Silicon
Logic is performed by resistors. Any positive input produces an inverted output irrespective of other inputs. Resistor R_b gives temperature stability.	The circuit design is straightforward. All logical operations can be performed with only this circuit. Many transistors readily meet the steady state requirements.	2N43A* 2N78* 2N167* 2N169A 2N396* 2N525 2N526* 2N635 2N1057	2N335*
Same as RTL except that capacitors are used to enhance switching speed. The capacitors increase the base current for fast collector current turn on and minimize storage time by supplying a charge equal to the stored base charge.	Faster than RTL at the expense of additional components and stringent stored charge requirements.	No standard types are characterized specifically for this logic 2N404* 2N525 2N634 2N1115	
Logic is performed by transistors. V_{CE} and V_{BE}, measured with the transistor in saturation, define the two logic levels. V_{CE} must be much less than V_{BE} to ensure stability and circuit flexibility.	Very low supply voltages may be used to achieve high power efficiency and miniaturization. Relatively fast switching speeds are practical.	4JD1A68 (PNP Alloy) Surface barrier types	
Logic is performed by diodes. The output is not inverted. Amplifiers are required to maintain the correct logic levels through several gates in series.	Several gates may be used between amplifiers. High speeds can be attained. Non-inversion simplifies circuit design problems. Relatively inexpensive components are used.	2N43A* 2N78* 2N123* 2N167* 2N396* 2N525 2N635	2N333* 2N337*
Logic is performed by diodes. The output is inverted. The diode D isolates the transistor from the gate permitting R to turn on the collector current. By proper choice of components only small voltage changes occur.	The number of inputs to the diode gate does not affect the transistor base current thus giving predictable performance. The small voltage excursions minimize the effects of stray capacitance and enhance switching speed.	2N123* 2N396* 2N525 2N526* 2N635 2N1115	2N335* 2N338*
Logic is performed by transistors which are biased from constant current sources to keep them far out of saturation. Both inverted and non-inverted outputs are available.	Very high switching speeds are possible because the transistors are operated at optimum operating conditions. Although the voltage excursion is small the circuitry is relatively unaffected by noise.	2N1289 Mesa Types	2N337* 2N338*

* Military types.

Logic systems.

signal *A*, is *absent*. Since the zero volts associated with the absent condition will not operate a circuit, another method must be used. This method is the use of an inverter circuit.

The output of an inverter is always the opposite of its input. Apply zero volts to its input and it will provide either a larger negative or a larger positive voltage at its output. Thus, if signal *A* is applied to an inverter, a *yes* or logical *1* output will be obtained when the *A* input is *no* or logical *0*. As will be recalled, the symbol *A* is usually used to represent the inverted form of signal $\overline{A}$.

	A	$\overline{A}$
CASE I	0	1
CASE 2	1	0

(A) Logic circuit. (B) Truth table.

Fig. 7-9. The inversion function.

When *A* is logical *0*, $\overline{A}$ (NOT A) is logical *1*. On the other hand, when *A* is logical *1*, $\overline{A}$ is logical *0*. These conditions are usually summarized in a form called a truth table, as shown in Fig. 7-9. Note that *A* and $\overline{A}$ can never be the same simultaneously. This follows when it is remembered that one is the inverted version of the other.

In many transistorized circuits the two logic functions, OR and AND, are passed through an inverter by necessity rather than choice. It will now be shown how inverted signals are used to perform useful functions.

Interchangeability Of *And* And *Or* Functions Using Inverted Signals

Many transistorized logic systems use inverting-OR circuits to perform both the OR and the AND function. This can be done only by using inverted signals. To understand how this is done, consideration must first be given to the possible ways in which an inverted-OR circuit can operate. The truth table in Fig. 7-10 shows these possibilities. The "F" column indicates the output of the circuit in each case. The table is derived by first writing down all possible combinations of inputs and then determining the output for each. For example, in *Cases 1* and *2* the output of the OR circuit will be logical *1* because one of the inputs is. However, the inverter will convert this to logical *0*. Consequently, the overall circuit output will be logical *0*. *Case 3* will also cause a logical *1* at the OR-circuit output and

96

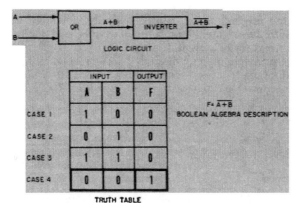

TRUTH TABLE

Fig. 7-10. The inverted-OR function.

will also appear at the inverter output as logical *0*. *Case 4* is different, since it produces a logical *0* at the OR-circuit output and a logical *1* at the inverter output.

Note that in *Case 4* a logical-*1* circuit output occurs when *both* inputs are logical *0*. When *A* and *B* are logical *0*, $\overline{A}$ and $\overline{B}$ are logical *1*. Thus, an AND function seems to be associated with the circuit. A positive-AND function will result if $\overline{A}$ and $\overline{B}$ are used as circuit inputs (Fig. 7-11).

Also note that $\overline{A} + \overline{B}$ is not the same as $\overline{A + B}$. If it were, the truth table would indicate that the underlined inverted version, $\overline{A} + \overline{B}$, was a positive-OR function because $\overline{A + B}$ (the second bar would be caused by the inverter) is equal to $A + B$. Stated electronically, a signal inverted twice comes back into phase

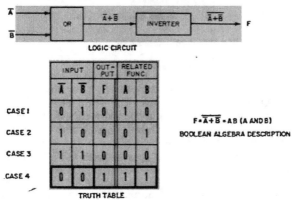

TRUTH TABLE

Fig. 7-11. The AND function using inverted-OR logic.

97

with the original signal. Stated logically, a double inversion results in the original input. It might even be said, jokingly, that two wrongs make a right.

This principle of providing an AND function using two inverted inputs to a negative-OR circuit is useful in applications where a few logic operations are cascaded (Fig. 7-12).

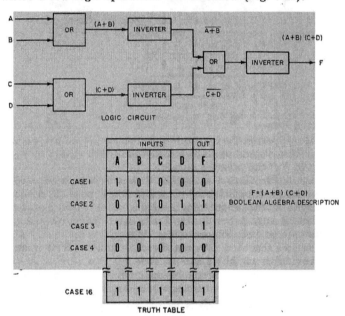

Fig. 7-12. Cascaded inverted-OR logic.

STATIC AND DYNAMIC LOGIC

The term *static logic* is often used to refer to logic circuits designed to operate with pulses that are fairly wide in relation to the system clock-pulses. The inputs to static logic are often the gate voltages from flip-flops. The logic circuits used in coding and decoding matrixes are usually considered as being static. Static logic is usually direct coupled and hence is also called *DC logic*.

Dynamic logic is designed to operate with the system clock-pulses being used as inputs and outputs. In some systems of dynamic logic, AC coupling-devices, such as capacitors and transformers, are used and hence these circuits are also called *AC logic*.

98

In some applications the same group of logic circuits can be used as static or dynamic. In the static mode of operation, logical inputs which cause a logical-1 output produce this output as long as the input conditions remain unchanged.

In the dynamic mode of operation, the logical inputs are AND-ed with a clock pulse. As a result, an output of logical 1 only occurs under the proper input conditions and then only when the clock pulse is present. This results in an output which only remains logical 1 for the short duration of the clock pulse.

Dynamic operation is usually used when data is to be transferred between parts of the computer. The pulses, being essentially AC, do not suffer the losses and distortion that wider pulses do. These wider pulses approach DC when considered in terms of the clock-pulse widths, stray capacitances, and inductances along the transmission wires. In serial systems using trains of pulses to represent data, delay lines are often used. The delay line is usually designed to process the narrow clock-pulses. If wider pulses are applied, the delay line often couples only the changing portions of the gate voltages (leading and trailing edges). Finally, the narrow pulses are often used for triggering flip-flops. Short trigger pulses are usually desired and so the logical conditions that are to result in triggering are used to gate a clock pulse to do the actual triggering.

In large data-processing systems, both static- and dynamic-logic techniques are used. The static techniques are used when there must be coincidence between fairly long gate voltages. Dynamic techniques are used for data transfer and triggering flip-flops. Note that static logic can process gate voltages of any width because it is direct coupled. On the other hand, dynamic-logic circuits are often designed to couple and respond to only pulses of a fixed and very narrow width (usually the clock-pulse width).

AND CIRCUITS

In digital computers, the AND circuit is any device which provides only a logical-1 output when each input is logical 1 (Fig. 7-13). As was noted earlier, there are many systems of logic which provide the AND function.

RTL AND Circuits

Resistor-Transistor Logic (RTL) AND circuits are created using negative-OR(NOR) or negative-AND(NAND) circuits in conjunction with stages of inversion. This is necessary because of the inversion produced by the associated transistors.

99

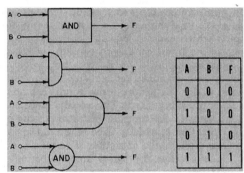

TYPICAL AND CIRCUIT SYMBOLS

A	B	F
0	0	0
1	0	0
0	1	0
1	1	1

TRUTH TABLE

Fig. 7-13. The AND circuit.

NOR-Circuit AND Configurations. The basic NOR circuit (Fig. 7-14) consists of series, current-limiting, and input resistors, as well as a grounded-emitter power transistor. The 15K resistor and −20-volt supply draw any cutoff current I_{co}, that might be developed by ambient temperature when the transistor is held at cutoff. This prevents base currents caused by thermal agitation from causing collector-current flow.

The transistor is held cutoff when all inputs are at approximately zero volts. This occurs because of the negative voltage on the base of the transistor. The transistor collector voltage is +20 volts at this time. As soon as *any* input voltage goes to +20 volts, the base becomes positive and a base current flows. The collector voltages change from +20 to approximately +0.25 volts.

An AND function is obtained using three NOR circuits (Fig. 7-15). In the logic configuration shown, both *A* and *B* must be logical *1* in order to provide an output of logical *1*.

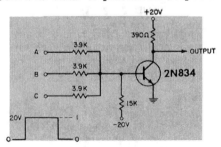

Fig. 7-14. A basic NOR circuit.

100

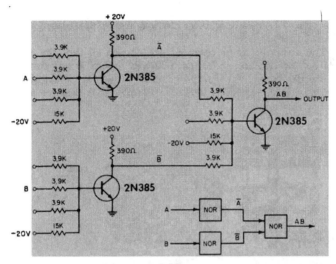

Fig. 7-15. A NOR AND circuit.

That is, the output NOR-circuit will provide a logical-*1* output as long as *both* inputs are logical *0*. Both inputs will be logical *0* only if the inputs to the two input NOR-circuits are logical *1* (*A* and *B*).

NAND-Circuit AND Configurations. The basic NAND circuit (Fig. 7-16) looks almost exactly like the NOR circuit, the major difference being in the values of the input base-current-limiting resistors. In the NAND circuit *all* inputs must be at logical *1* before the associated power transistor conducts. As a result, in the case shown each input provides one-third of the current required to cause the transistor base voltage to become

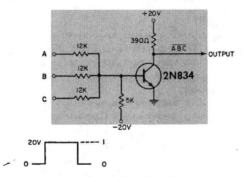

Fig. 7-16. A basic NAND circuit.

101

positive. The resulting base current causes transistor conduction.

The value of input resistors are chosen so that the current caused by two simultaneous +20-volt inputs is not enough to cause the base voltage to go positive. However, when all three inputs are at +20 volts, the base voltage goes positive and the transistor conducts.

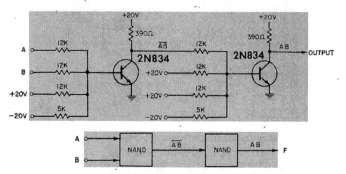

Fig. 7-17. A NAND AND circuit.

It is very important to note that all inputs must be present in order to operate the NAND circuit. In applications where only one or two logical-NAND inputs are required, the remaining inputs must be connected to a source of +20 volts DC. In the case of the NOR circuit, all unused inputs must be grounded in order to insure proper circuit operation.

A NAND-circuit configuration that will perform the AND function is shown in Fig. 7-17. Here, the second NAND circuit merely acts as an inverter.

RCTL AND Circuits

Resistor-Capacitor-Transistor Logic (RCTL) circuits are almost identical to RTL circuits (Fig. 7-18). RCTL circuits, however, have capacitors which parallel the series input resistances. These speed-up capacitors reduce the rise and fall time of the associated transistor.

During transistor turn-on, the speed-up capacitors bypass the current-limiting resistors and provide a peak overdrive base-current. This occurs during the leading edge of the input gate-voltage. After the capacitors charge, the base current is supplied through the resistor. During transistor turn-off, the speed-up capacitor minimizes the storage time by supplying the excess current required to draw the majority carriers

102

from the base region and the stored charge from the collector region.

The value of the required bypass capacitance is computed in two ways. The first method makes use of the following relationship:

$$C = \frac{i\Delta t}{\Delta V_{in}}$$

This equation states that the value of required capacitance is equal to the drive current multiplied by the rise (or fall) time and divided by the input-voltage swing. This method can be applied to any transistor.

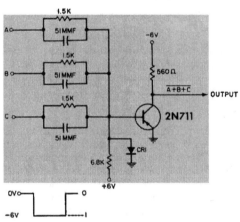

Fig. 7-18. An RCTL NOR circuit.

The second method makes use of data concerning a specific type of transistor. For example, the Motorola Semiconductor Products Corporation provides a graph which indicates the amount of the excess charge in the 2N711 transistor as a function of the base current flowing before turn-off. The capacitance required to draw out this charge (to allow rapid turn-off) is computed using the value of excess charge known to exist (Fig. 7-19).

Base control-charge consists of the sum of the excess carriers in the base region *plus* the stored charge in the collector region *plus* the additional charge required to bring the transistor to the turn-off region. During turn-off, the voltage stored in the bypass capacitor causes a discharge current which flows through the emitter-base junction (in the reverse direction)

103

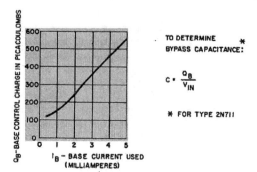

TO DETERMINE *
BYPASS CAPACITANCE:

$$C = \frac{Q_B}{V_{IN}}$$

* FOR TYPE 2N711

Fig. 7-19. Base-control-charge curve to compute bypass-capacitance value needed in RCTL circuits.

and literally "draws out" the undesirable charges created during transistor conduction and which delay turn-off.

RCTL NOR and NAND circuits are used to provide the AND function in the same manner as the RTL circuits.

DCTL AND Circuits

A Direct-Coupled Transistor Logic (DCTL) AND circuit (Fig. 7-20) consists of series-connected transistors which perform the *not*-AND function, and an inverter circuit to convert the *not*-AND function into the AND function.

The AND Function. When all inputs are logical *1*, all series transistors conduct and the output voltage goes from logical *1* to logical *0*. The inverter output then goes from logical *0* to

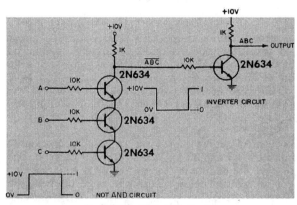

Fig. 7-20. A DCTL AND circuit.

logical *1*. As a result, the entire circuit performs the AND function. The series-connected transistors act as a group of series-connected switches. For example, if input *C* is the only input at logical *1*, base current will flow but the collector voltage is zero because of the high resistance of the other non-conducting series transistors. As a result, no collector current flows and the overall circuit is unchanged.

When input *A* becomes logical *1* and inputs *B* and *C* are logical *0*, the high resistance of the non-conducting transistors in series with the emitter prevents appreciable base-current flow. Consequently, collector current does not flow in the upper transistor. When input *B* becomes logical *1* and input *C* is logical *0*, base current is also limited. However, when all three transistors are gated *on* by inputs of logical *1*, base and collector resistances are almost zero and both base and collector current flows.

The OR Function. It is interesting to note that the same circuit used to provide an AND function can be used to perform the OR function also if the inputs are inverted and the *not*-AND ouput is not inverted.

In the circuit shown, the logical *1* is indicated by +10 volts. Consider what will happen if the inputs are inverted before they are applied to the circuit (Fig. 7-21). That is, if $\bar{A}$, $\bar{B}$, and $\bar{C}$ were used to operate the AND circuit even though *A*, *B*, and *C* were applied. Thus, all transistors of the *not*-AND circuit will conduct (logical-*0* output) when all inputs (*A*, *B*, and *C*) are logical *0*. This occurs because the *inverted* inputs are all logical *1*. In addition, if any input becomes logical *1*, the inverted version becomes logical *0*. As a result, the associated *not*-AND-circuit transistor becomes cutoff. This in turn causes the *not*-AND circuit to provide a logical-*1* output of +10 volts. As indicated by the truth table, this results in the OR function being performed.

As a general rule, when the inputs are inverted a *not*-AND circuit becomes an OR circuit. It follows then that when all inputs are inverted, a *not*-OR circuit will become an AND circuit.

DL *AND* Circuits

The Diode Logic (DL) AND circuit can be achieved in two ways. When *positive* voltages are used to represent logical *1*, and zero volts represents logical *0*, one configuration (positive AND) is used. When *negative* voltages represent logical *1*, and zero volts represents logical *0*, the second configuration (negative AND) is used.

The Positive DL AND Circuit. The positive diode logic (DL) AND circuit (Fig. 7-22) consists of diodes and a common resistor. When all inputs are at logical *0* (approximately zero volts), the output is logical *0* (about 1 volt). The input is shown as actually having a lower value of +0.4 volt which represents the lower output voltage of a conducting transistor. Most conducting transistors will provide a voltage of this approximate

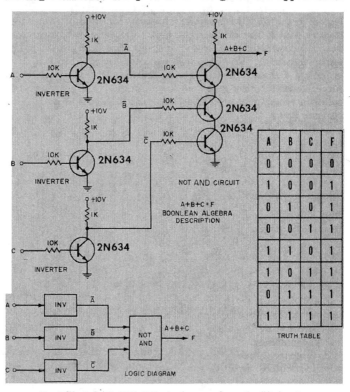

Fig. 7-21. A DCTL NOT AND circuit to perform the OR function.

value. In addition, the circuit shown has been designed to maintain approximately +0.6 volt across each diode when all are conducting. As a result, the total drop between the plate of each conducting diode and ground is approximately 1 volt.

When any input becomes logical *1* (+10 volts), the associated diode is cut off because the plate is held near ground potential by the other still-conducting diodes. When all inputs become

106

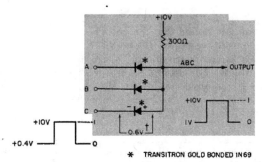

Fig. 7-22. A positive DL AND circuit.

logical *1*, however, all of the associated diodes are cut off and the AND-circuit output rises to almost +10 volts (logical *1*). When all of the diodes are cut off, the output voltage is determined by the voltage divider consisting of the 300-ohm resistor and the load resistance.

Note that each time one of the input diodes become cut off, the remaining diodes conduct a higher current and undergo a slight increase in the voltage drop across them. Thus, the lower output voltage may actually vary by a few hundredths of a volt as a result of inputs becoming logical *1*.

The Negative DL AND Circuit. The negative DL AND circuit (Fig. 7-23) operates in much the same way as the positive one. The only difference is that the negative AND circuit responds to logical-*1* conditions represented by a negative voltage.

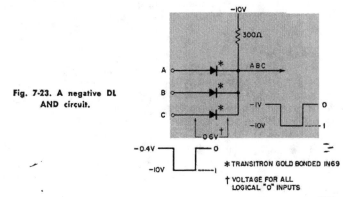

Fig. 7-23. A negative DL AND circuit.

107

DIODE VOLTAGE DROPS

It has been mentioned that the voltage drop across the diodes affect the output voltages. It should also be noted that the voltage drop across germanium diodes varies as a result of input conditions. For example, in the AND circuits shown, there are four possible conditions, each causing different voltage drops across them. The approximate values for the circuits shown are as follows:

Condition	Voltage Across Each Diode	Current Through Each Diode
All Diodes Conducting	0.6 volts	10 milliamperes
Two Diodes Conducting	0.7 volts	15 milliamperes
One Diode Conducting	1.0 volt	30 milliamperes

The total output voltage of a diode circuit is the algebraic sum of the input voltage and the voltage across the diode. Most inputs are obtained from the collector of a transistor. Thus, the lower-level input corresponds to the near-saturation collector voltage. This voltage is usually from 0.1 to 0.4 volts. The diode configuration and the polarity of the low-level collector voltage (logical 0) determine whether the voltage at the output of the circuit is the sum or the difference between the low-level input voltage and the voltage drop across the diode.

OR CIRCUITS

In digital computers, the OR circuit is any device which provides a logical-1 output when any input becomes logical 1 (Fig. 7-24).

RTL OR Circuits

Resistor-Transistor Logic (RTL) OR circuits are created using the NOR circuit in conjunction with stages of inversion. As mentioned in the discussion of RTL AND circuits, the basic NOR circuit consists of a few inputs (Fig. 7-25) to a cutoff transistor. When any input becomes logical 1 (+12 volts in the circuit shown), the base voltage becomes positive and the transistor conducts. Inversion occurs because the collector voltage of the associated transistor goes from logical 1 (+12 volts), which was present during cutoff, to a few tenths of a volt (logical 0) during conduction. Since the collector voltage goes

108

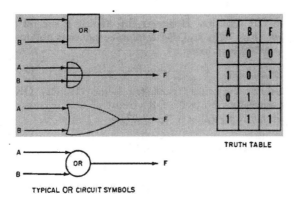

A	B	F
0	0	0
1	0	1
0	1	1
1	1	1

TRUTH TABLE

TYPICAL OR CIRCUIT SYMBOLS

Fig. 7-24. The OR circuit.

Fig. 7-25. A basic NOR circuit.

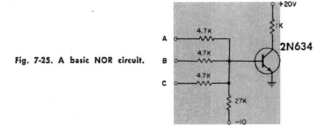

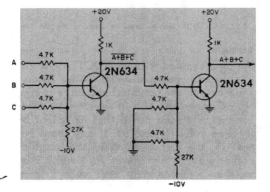

Fig. 7-26. RTL NOR circuits used to perform the OR function.

109

to logical *0* when any input becomes logical *1*, the output is an inverted OR function. However, by adding a second stage of inversion (Fig. 7-26) an OR-function response is obtained when any input becomes logical *1*.

RCTL OR Circuits

A Resistor-Capacitor-Transistor Logic (RCTL) OR circuit is very similar to the RTL OR circuit in that it consists of an inverted NOR function (Fig. 7-27).

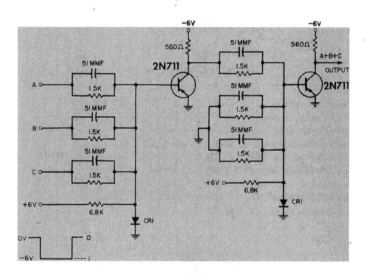

Fig. 7-27. RCTL NOR circuits used to perform the OR function.

DCTL OR Circuits

Direct-Coupled Transistor Logic (DCTL) OR circuits work on a parallel-switch principle (Fig. 7-28). When all of the transistors are cut off, the potential at point *a* is approximately +10 volts. This causes the output inverter to draw base current and conduct, with the result that its output becomes approximately zero volts (logical *0*). If any input becomes +10 volts (logical *1*), the associated transistor conducts and bypasses the other parallel transistors. As a result, the voltage at point *a* becomes approximately zero volts (logical *0*). This cuts off the inverter and causes its collector to change to approximately +10 volts (logical *1*).

110

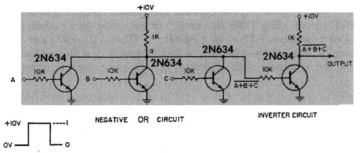

Fig. 7-28. A DCTL OR circuit.

DL OR Circuits

Diode Logic (DL) OR circuits are identical to DL AND circuits. However, the operation depends upon the input polarity. The positive OR circuit is the same as the negative AND circuit, and the negative OR circuit is the same as the positive AND circuit.

The Positive DL OR Circuit. The positive DL OR circuit (Fig. 7-29) provides an output of approximately zero volts (logical 0) when all inputs are approximately zero volts (logical 0). However, when any one of the inputs becomes logical 1 (+10 volts), the current drawn by that input causes the OR-

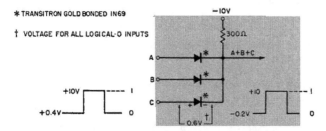

Fig. 7-29. A positive DL OR circuit.

circuit output to become approximately +10 volts (logical 1). Looking at it another way, when the diode is forward biased it connects the +10 volts at the input to the output in much the way that a small-value series resistor would. The diodes associated with the zero-volt inputs, however, are cutoff at this time because the cathodes are more positive than the plates. That is, the other diodes are reverse biased and act as open switches.

111

The Negative DL OR Circuit. The output of the negative DL OR circuit (Fig. 7-30) becomes −10 volts (logical *1*) when any input becomes −10 volts (logical *1*). When all inputs are logical *0* (approximately zero volts), the output voltage consists of the algebraic sum of the input voltage (from the collector

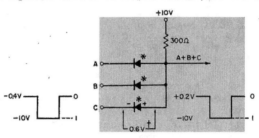

* TRANSITRON GOLD BONDED IN69

† VOLTAGE FOR ALL LOGICAL·0 INPUTS

Fig. 7-30. A negative DL OR circuit.

of the preceding stage) and the voltage drop across each diode. When an input becomes logical *1* (−10 volts), the −10 volts is coupled through the associated diode to the output. The other diodes are cut off.

REVIEW QUESTIONS

1. What do the following Boolean algebra notations mean?
   a. A, B, C
   b. AB
   c. A + B
   d. $\bar{A}$ + B
   e. A$\bar{B}$

2. What is the main circuit feature of resistor-transistor logic (RTL)?

3. What is the main circuit feature of resistor-capacitor-transistor logic (RCTL)?

4. What is the main circuit feature of direct-coupled transistor logic (DCTL)?

5. What is the main circuit feature of diode logic (DL)?

6. What is the main circuit feature of low-level logic (LLL)?

7. What is the main circuit feature of current-mode logic (CML)?

8. What is the relationship between A and $\bar{A}$?

9. Why can an inverted OR circuit be used to perform the AND function?

10. What basic logic circuit is used to provide both the AND and the OR function?

112

CHAPTER 8

Flip Flops

A data-processing device (any form of computer) is made possible by its ability to make a *decision*. In other words, it must be able to compare two elements of data, for example, to determine which is greater or less than the other—and to do something with that decision (store it, or add it to some other data). Even with this oversimplification, it can readily be seen that the machine must handle more than one item of data—specifically two in the case given. These decisions are ridiculously simple in their basic concept, such as, *is the light switch ON or OFF?* (If the light switch is similar to the ones found in most homes, it would only be necessary to look to see if the switch lever is UP, and if so, it would be known the light is ON. Of course, the lamp could be observed to see if it was lit, but *that* would be cheating!)

Agreed, then, the machine needs a choice of on-off, yes-no, true-false, or *a choice of any two possibilities at all*. To supply this electronically, it is only necessary to provide a circuit output of + or −, then select which practical problem choice is to be labelled + and which −. If this was done, the one circuit could handle all the logic situations that might arise. A flip-flop is an electronic circuit that can fulfill these requirements.

BASIC PRINCIPLE OF FLIP-FLOPS

The flip-flop is a circuit with two possible outputs (two possible decisions), shown in Fig. 8-1 as F and $\overline{F}$, (also called logical 1 or 0, + or −). The important points to remember are (1) there are two opposite outputs, and (2) the type of information fed into the circuit will determine which of the outputs will be provided at any given instant. The symbols in Fig. 8-1 show a number of ways in which the flip-flop may appear in schematic logic presentations.

Functional Description of Flip-Flop

Note that the first logic symbol in Fig. 8-1 shows *FF* in the center, identifying that logic block as a flip-flop. Note also that three inputs are possible—Set, Reset, and Complement. Set and Reset are pretty much the same, except that Set

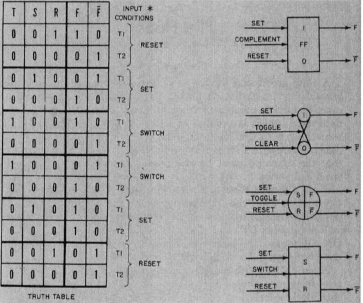

T	S	R	F	F̄	INPUT * CONDITIONS	
0	0	1	1	0	T1	RESET
0	0	0	0	1	T2	
0	1	0	0	1	T1	SET
0	0	0	1	0	T2	
1	0	0	1	0	T1	SWITCH
0	0	0	0	1	T2	
1	0	0	0	1	T1	SWITCH
0	0	0	1	0	T2	
0	1	0	1	0	T1	SET
0	0	0	1	0	T2	
0	0	1	0	1	T1	RESET
0	0	0	0	1	T2	

TRUTH TABLE

*NOTE:
TI IS THE TIME THAT THE INPUT PULSE IS APPLIED. T2 IS A TIME A FEW TENTHS OF A MICRO SECOND LATER WHEN THE INPUT PULSE IS REMOVED AND THE FLIP–FLOP HAS OPERATED. THE FLIP–FLOP REMAINS IN THE STATE AT T2 UNTIL ANOTHER INPUT PULSE IS APPLIED.

LOGIC SYMBOLS

Fig. 8-1. Flip-flop logic.

triggers a *1* output, and Reset triggers a *0*. (Of course, if the circuit was at the desired output at the start of the signal input, the applied signal would not change anything). Complement is a unique function, representing the input which makes the circuit do a complete reversal of states, so that *whichever* logical output was present previously will be exactly reversed.

The second logic box shows logical *1* as the upper symbol, with the Set input representing a particular signal (such as +) applied to the logical-*1* side. This "sets" the circuit, so that a

114

logical *1* appears at the output. If the Clear input is applied to the logical-*0* side, the circuit is "cleared" and a logical *0* appears at the *F* output. The Toggle input complements the circuit, making the output the reverse of what it was before.

The next two logic symbols shown are simply graphic variations of the first two, with identical logical functions. Any of these symbols might be used in a schematic of a computer logic circuit.

The word flip-flop means simply that the circuit will switch very rapidly from one output (say logical *1*) to the opposite (say logical *0*) when the appropriate input signal is applied. It could be said the output voltage *flips* to positive, then *flops* to negative, upon command. It's simply an electronic switch whose output is either *On* or *Off* depending upon the logic required— really not much different from the On-Off switch on the wall, except that the result is electronic, rather than visual.

Study the truth table in Fig. 8-1 and observe the behavior of the flip-flop as a logic device. Use the upper logic symbol in the illustration as a guide. The truth-table headings are: T for toggle (complement), S for set, R for reset, F and $\bar{F}$ for outputs. Consider the facts in the first line of the table: T is logical *0* (there is *no complement* input), S is logical *0* (there is *no set* input), and R is logical *1*, (there is a *positive reset* signal input). The condition of F (representing the logical-*1* output), is logical *1*, hence $\bar{F}$ (representing the other output) must automatically be at the logical-*0* state. All these conditions are at time *T1* (the instant the input signal is applied).

Look now at the second line of the table. *T2* represents an instant after the input signal has been applied. The T and S inputs have not been affected, since nothing had been applied before. The R input now falls to logical *0* (no pulse), since the input pulse has passed. Now consider the output F and $\bar{F}$, remembering that the outputs *after* the switching action has taken place is being inspected. Since the reset pulse automatically brings the logical-*1* output side to *0*, F is logical *0*. The $\bar{F}$ output, by definition, must flop over to its opposite polarity whenever the circuit switches, so $\bar{F}$ is logical *1*.

Of course, it was assumed that the *F*-output side was at the logical-*1* condition at the beginning of this operation. Suppose it had been at the logical-*0* condition instead? The last two lines of the table shows the same operation, but with the *F* output starting at the logical-*0* condition. Note that the resultant outputs are exactly the same, since the function of the reset pulse is to *clear* the *F* output and make it logical *0*, *no matter what it had been* before.

Similarly, it will be found that the third and fourth lines of the truth table show the Set operation, with F equal to logical 1 as the ultimate result. Note that the alternate Set operation (lines 9 and 10 in the table) provides the same result as when F was assumed to be at the opposite state at the beginning. The two *switch* cases in the table show the *complementing* action when a switch (or toggle) pulse is applied. This action reverses the outputs, no matter what they had been before.

BI-STABLE OPERATION

The switching action of the flip-flop lends itself particularly well to bi-stable operation. Fig. 8-2 shows a multivibrator circuit with two transistors whose outputs are cross-coupled. (Note the typical appearance of the X-shaped cross-coupling in the diagram. It will help to spot a flip-flop every time). The

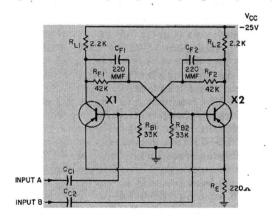

Fig. 8-2. A saturated flip-flop circuit.

built-in circuit stability, which keeps one transistor switched on and the other switched off, distinguishes the bi-stable flip-flop from the oscillating multivibrator. When the off transistor is triggered by the appropriate input pulse, it is switched on. This starts a chain reaction, which ends when the opposite transistor is switched off. This now becomes the new stable state and remains so until a new input pulse triggers the circuit. Since the flip-flop can be stable in either of the two states, it is frequently called a bi-stable multivibrator. (Certain other modes of flip-flop operation are possible, including mono-stable or single-shot. These, however, are not of particular concern

116

at this time). The conventional bi-stable circuit may be further classified as *saturating* or *non-saturating*, with particular advantages to each mode.

Saturated-Mode Flip-Flop

Note that the two transistors in Fig. 8-2 have their emitters essentially grounded (220 ohms above ground), so they can be expected to act as inverters. (It has sometimes been stated that a flip-flop is nothing more than two inverters, back-to-back and cross-coupled). For this analysis, disregard the logic functions of inputs and outputs, and consider only the electronic circuitry. The logic will be covered after this analysis.

Consider X1 as being cut off at the start of operation. Its output resistance is now very high, making the collector current practically zero. There is, however, a current flow through the voltage-divider network consisting of resistors R_{L1}, R_{F1}, and R_{B2} that are connected between V_{cc} and ground. This causes voltage drops across each resistor. (For the analytically-minded, the exact drops can be figured by applying Ohm's law. Otherwise, use the approximate figures which follow.) The drop across R_{L1} equals 0.7 volt, leaving practically the full −25 volts at the collector of X1. Since R_{F1} is about 20 times larger than R_{L1}, its drop is approximately 14 volts. By similar proportion, R_{B2} will have a drop of about 10.3 volts. With −10.3 volts at the base of X2 (the on transistor), that transistor is strongly forward-biased, and will plunge into saturation. Emitter current flowing through R_E places both emitters at about −2 volts. This does not interfere with the forward-bias action of X2, but it places its base at about −2 volts. This changes, somewhat, the voltage-divider action of R_{L1} and R_{F1}. In addition, R_{B2} is effectively bypassed since the base-emitter diode now has a lower-resistance path than R_{B2}.

The saturated collector of X2 draws a heavy current through its load resistor R_{L2}, causing a drop of about 23 volts across it, leaving the X2 collector at about −2 volts. The voltage-divider resistors, R_{F2} and R_{B1}, divide the −2 volts proportionately, so that a little over −1 volt is applied to the base of X1. Since the X1 emitter is at about −2 volts, it remains cut off, maintaining the stable condition found at the start of operation.

Suppose now that a negative-going trigger pulse is applied at input A through coupling-capacitor C_{C1}, to the base of X1 (the off transistor). If the pulse is sufficiently negative to forward-bias the emitter-base junction, current will flow and switch X1 on. By following the explanation previously given for the switched-on transistor, you can readily note that the

117

switching action is carried through to the point where X2 is switched off, establishing the new stable state. (Of course, a positive triggering pulse at input B would do the same thing, by turning X2 off.)

Speed-up capacitors, C_{F1} and C_{F2}, act to rapidly couple the regenerative voltage-change from the voltage-dividers to the appropriate transistor bases to ensure rapid switching action. Remember, the charging action of a capacitor in parallel with a resistance is such that the *rate* of voltage change through the capacitor is *much greater* than the rate of change through the resistor at the beginning of the change cycle. The time constant of the parallel capacitor-resistor combination determines the fall time (from conduction to cutoff) of the transistor being cut off.

Other special applications of saturated flip-flops include direct-coupled circuits (to simplify and economize on circuit operation) and transistor-element circuits (where transistors replace the coupling elements, such as resistors, to speed up circuit operation). It's curious to note that although it would seem that cutting out components would make the circuit faster, transistor flip-flops generally operate fastest with maximum complex design containing as many as eight transistors.

Saturated Flip-Flop with Logic

The conventional flip-flop of Fig. 8-2 has been re-drawn in Fig. 8-3, with circuit values omitted for simplicity (they are exactly the same as the other illustration), but with the logic connections shown. Compare the input and output connections with the logic block at the top of Fig. 8-1 and the similarity will be evident. The output from the collector of X1 is the logical-*1*, or F output. The output from the collector of X2 is the logical-*0*, or $\overline{F}$ output. Since these collectors are always at opposite extremes of current (one transistor always on and one off), the logical outputs will always be at opposite extremes of signal. The two inputs (originally A and B) are now the Set and Reset. Input S sets X1 to a logical-*1* output by feeding in a negative pulse to its base. Input R resets X2 to a logical-*0* output by feeding the same kind of a negative pulse to its base. The complementary input T (toggle) provides a path for the same kind of negative input pulse through coupling capacitor C_{C3} to the negative side of diodes S_{D1} and S_{D2}. This permits the negative-going input pulse to be applied directly to *both* transistor bases. No matter which transistor is conducting, they *both* are given the triggering pulse, but only the one in the off condition is affected (turned on) effectively complementing

118

the previous output signal. Diodes S_{D1} and S_{D2} could be even more efficient if they were connected into the circuit as *steering* diodes.

The input signal can be *steered* into selective signal-paths by the use of strategically located directional diodes. (See Fig. 8-4). There is a subtlety in the use of steering diodes. It might be asked, "Why not isolate the two input bases with appropriate coupling capacitors and feed a common input signal to *both* bases? Why use special steering diodes?" The fact is, such a circuit *would work*, but switching time would be delayed. In computer applications the cry is, "Faster, faster!" The steering diode helps.

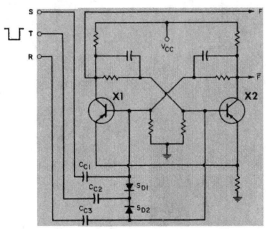

Fig. 8-3. A flip-flop with all logic connections.

If a negative input pulse is applied to the bases of both transistors from a common input source (isolated by capacitors to avoid DC interaction), the tendency for circuit operation would be for the off transistor to be driven into *conduction* (that's *good*), and the on transistor into *saturation* (that's *bad*). Of course, the turning-on action of the previously-off transistor prevails—but it must bring the previously-on transistor out of saturation. It must also bring it out of the even *deeper* state caused by the additional bias provided by the common input pulse. This calls for increased signal-voltage swing (a function of time), so that the resultant regeneration and transition time is similarly slowed up.

How do the pulse-steering diodes help? Assume the desired input pulse is negative. See Fig. 8-4A. The pulse passes through

119

coupling capacitor C_c, and through the voltage-divider R1-R2, which had been keeping the cathodes of the diodes at a positive potential. Diode C_{R1} has been back-biased, because the on transistor, say X2, has a significant negative base-voltage. For comparable reasons, C_{R2} has been conducting because of its forward bias. Thus, when the negative trigger-pulse comes through C_c, reverse-biased C_{R1} prevents the pulse from being applied to the base of the on transistor. Forward-biased diode

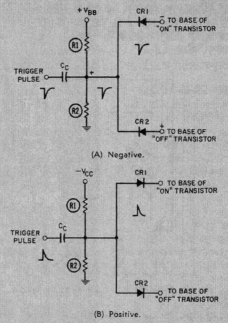

(A) Negative.

(B) Positive.

Fig. 8-4. Pulse-steering diode circuits.

C_{R2}, however, permits the negative trigger-pulse to pass through easily, and to be applied to the base of X1, turning it on in the conventional fashion. After the switching action, the pulse-steering diodes change bias accordingly, so that the *next* trigger pulse would be blocked by C_{R2}, but would easily pass through C_{R1}. Note also that a positive trigger-pulse applied to this steering circuit, regardless of the state of the flip-flop, *increases* the reverse bias on the diodes, and hence has no triggering effect on the circuit.

For positive-connected pulse-steering (used with NPN transistors) the circuit would be set up as in Fig. 8-4B. Note that

120

the voltage-divider polarity is reversed, and the steering-diode directions are changed.

The insistent need for greater circuit-switching speed dictates the use of pulse-steering diodes in saturating flip-flops, where the resultant switching speeds are acceptable. Where even faster operation is required, the transistor is prevented from going into saturation even when switching on. This mode is called nonsaturating flip-flop operation.

Nonsaturating Flip-Flop

To prevent the transistor from going into saturation, lower and upper limits are established for the output voltage in both stable states, keeping the *voltage swing* down to the minimum required for reliable switching. This increases the pulse repeti-

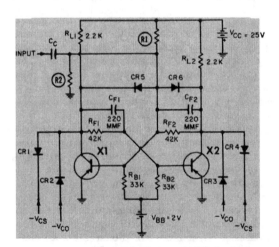

Fig. 8-5. A non-saturating flip-flop with diode clamping and positive pulse steering.

tion rate. Diode-clamps C_{R1} and C_{R2}, in Fig. 8-5, provide saturation clamping and cutoff clamping, respectively, for transistor X1. Similarly, C_{R3} and C_{R4} on the opposite side of the circuit provides cutoff and saturation clamping for X2. Consider X1 with its applicable diode clamps. The emitter-base junction is reverse biased by battery V_{BB} through base resistor R_{B1}. Collector reverse bias is provided by battery V_{CO} through load resistor R_{L1}. If X1 is on, it is because something makes its base negative enough with respect to the X1 emitter (ground) to overcome the reverse bias. At this time X1 would turn on

121

making its collector draw current heavily. As the X1 collector voltage (originally at −25 volts) starts to approach ground potential (representing transistor saturation), C_{R1} becomes forward-biased, clamping the collector at a voltage just short of saturation. This allows it to switch on as required. When circuit conditions cause X1 to turn off, the collector voltage starts to go negative (approaching −25 volts as supplied by V_{CC}). Now, C_{R2} starts to conduct, clamping the collector at the edge of cutoff so as to require less of a signal swing to turn it on later. Thus, C_{R1} and C_{R2}, pointing in opposite directions, determine both the turn-on and turn-off points for the transistor. In similar fashion, C_{R3} and C_{R4} clamps X2. This makes the flip-flop a non-saturating type.

Positive pulse-steering is provided by the voltage-divider action of R1 and R2 connected between V_{CC} and ground, with C_{R5} and C_{R6} acting as steering diodes. Note that now the positive input pulse turns off the collector of the on transistor. The original flip-flop is now becoming a little more complex, but it still can be related to the logical block of Fig. 8-1. All that is needed is: (1) a Set input-line through a coupling capacitor to the X1 base, (2) a Reset input-line through a coupling capacitor to the X2 base, (3) a logical *1* output from the collector of X1, and (4) a logical *0* output from the X2 collector.

In the timeless race for faster circuitry, new transistor geometry and new manufacturing techniques permit reduced carrier storage and more rapid switching in circuits which take advantage of the transistor capabilities. A slight circuit economy and a marked increase in switching speed is made possible by the differentiating action of steering-diode circuitry, as shown in the partial schematic diagram of Fig. 8-6. Only the complementary input is shown, with signal paths to both NPN transistor bases. The remainder of the circuit would be exactly the same as the other diagrams show. The base resistors, R_{B1} and R_{B2}, return to −6 volts. The on transistor has a predominantly positive base (to permit forward bias) so S_{D1} has its cathode essentially positive, thus acting back-biased to any positive pulse at the input. The off-transistor base is predominantly negative (for back-biasing) so S_{D2} is forward-biased for a positive input pulse. (This was discussed in the paragraph on steering diodes.) Note, however, the point common to both steering diodes is at the junction of C and R. These components form a differentiating circuit for the input pulse. The RC time constant is chosen so as to utilize the rising portion of the square-wave input (arrow pointing up between A and B of the input waveform) to provide a steep positive spike of short

122

duration to pass through the steering diode (S_{D2} in this case) for fastest switching-action. Since this type of differentiating circuit is generally used in circuits where a pulse train (rather than a single or an occasional pulse) is repetitively provided, the dotted portion of the waveform after differentiation is also shown. The negative spike simply back-biases the steering diodes further, however, and does not affect circuit operation

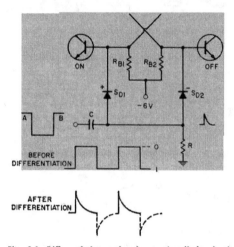

Fig. 8-6. Differentiating action in steering-diode circuits.

at all. (Remember this unique effect of differentiating action whenever steering diodes are seen biased for a *positive* input pulse, with a *negative*-going trigger provided by the designer!)

FLIP-FLOP LOGIC

With the explanation of the electronic operation of the flip-flop accomplished, thinking both electronically and logically when dealing with logic circuitry should be easier. Most of the language of computers is spoken and written in logic block diagrams, as shown in Fig. 8-7. The representation of the AND and FLIP-FLOP logic blocks have already been explained. Here, they are seen working together in a very simple logic circuit. (The schematic diagram for this type of logic circuit is found in the next chapter.) The AND block has two inputs, the lower of which is the signal to start the little theoretical machine working. However, it does not matter how frequently a signal is fed into the input because the AND circuit will not

123

pass it unless the upper input is also available. Since a single input-signal frequently supplies a number of AND gates, a convention has been followed in this illustration by having the upper input coincide with the upper line of the AND block. In this way, the same line could continue on to other blocks, *conditioning* them so that they are ready to receive the other input required for coincidence operation.

Suppose, for instance, the AND block has been conditioned by a signal from the upper input. The signal input from the lower line now operates the AND circuit and provides an output to the first flip-flop. Note that both flip-flops, though electrically constructed the same, use certain optional inputs and

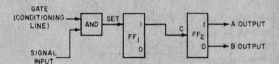

Fig. 8-7. A combination of AND and flip-flop logic.

outputs. These will be ignored since they are not used in this case. Thus, FF_1 uses only one input, the Set, which when triggered by the preceding AND circuit sets the logical-1 output. This, in turn, now acts as the complementary input to FF_2, switching it so that the outputs (A and B) now have opposite polarities from what they had before. Nothing significant will happen to this machine until conditions at the first AND block start the train of events again, once more complementing the A and B outputs of FF_2.

Simple Register Logic

The logic circuitry becomes more sophisticated as a group of flip-flops are arranged in a certain order, permitting their logical outputs to be *read* as a group of *bits,* forming a *word.* Thus, in Fig. 8-8, FF_1, FF_2, and FF_3 comprise *Register A*, permitting any combination of logical bits from *000* to *111*. (The schematic diagram for this type of logic circuit is found in the next chapter.) In the simple register logic shown, only the logical-1 outputs are used. Each output actuates an associated AND gate *when the AND gate is conditioned* by a signal from the gate-conditioning line. (Note that the conditioning line appears at the top line of the AND block.) The outputs of the AND gates complement the flip-flops of register B, providing an output *word* of 3 bits, which are now available to other logic circuitry to accomplish other data processing. Of course the

124

logical-0 outputs of any or all of these flip-flops could be used for some other logic function at the same time. However, only a simple version of a logical operation has been shown. A truly complex machine has lines criss-crossing all over, but they can be traced as simply as this circuit if a methodical tracing procedure is followed.

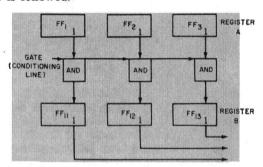

Fig. 8-8. Simple register logic.

If the electronic circuitry involved in the logic of Fig. 8-8, is puzzling, look for it in the detailed review of combination flip-flop-AND circuitry in counters, described in the following chapter. It is important to *speak* in both the electronic-design language of circuitry and in the computer-design language of logic blocks. Individual logic blocks become gates and flip-flops, groups become counters, and larger groups become registers. In this manner, they build up into the largest data-processing machines.

REVIEW QUESTIONS

1. What is a flip-flop?

2. What is the characteristic connection of a flip-flop?

3. How can a flip-flop be considered in terms of inverters?

4. What are speed-up capacitors used for?

5. What are steering diodes used for?

6. How are transistor flip-flops kept from going into saturation?

7. What is register logic?

CHAPTER 9

Counters and Shift Registers

When a child is asked to count, he starts touching his fingers and recites the number which he attaches mentally to each. When he gets to ten, he has to start with the first finger all over again (or take off his shoes and count his toes). Because most data-processing circuits have only "two fingers" (two stable states), counting is performed in units of *two*, with the flip-flop as the *binary* counting-element.

BINARY COUNTERS

Fig. 9-1 shows three flip-flops in tandem. The upper portion is the logic diagram and the lower portion the schematic. Only the first flip-flop is detailed schematically. Those following are simplified to show the significant electronic paths. By making reference to the logic diagrams and to the schematic circuitry as required, it should be possible to follow the binary-counter operation without difficulty.

The first flip-flop (FF_1) is called the *lowest-order* counter to which the input signal-pulse is applied (at the complementary input). Every time a flip-flop (FF_1 for instance) changes from a logical-1 to a logical-0 output (note that the 0 output is of particular significance in this design), a trigger signal is sent to the next higher-order counter (FF_2). The flip-flop output level (logical 0) is coupled to trigger the complementary input of FF_2. Exactly the same operation, as explained above, occurs in FF_2 and in all the succeeding flip-flops. Now, how can this counter be used practically?

Binary Counting

Fig. 9-2 shows single-bit counting with a four flip-flop counter. Note that the input pulse is applied at the *right*. This permits showing the resultant binary total as it would be read by an observer. The top row shows the counter at the beginning of the operation. Imagine the output with pilot-lamp indicators (many do have). The total, both in binary and in the decimal equivalent, equals zero. The binary counting sequence is as follows:

1. Look at the second row. The first pulse has been applied. This complements FF_1, lighting the logical-1 output. It has been agreed that in this counter, every time the output of a flip-flop changes from a logical 1 to a logical 0 a pulse is sent to the next higher-order counter. Since the only counter action in this operation has been a change from logical 0 to logical 1, no output pulse is generated. (Of course the logical-0 output transmits a level to FF_1, but the polarity is not correct to trigger it.) Note that binary 0001 equals decimal 1.

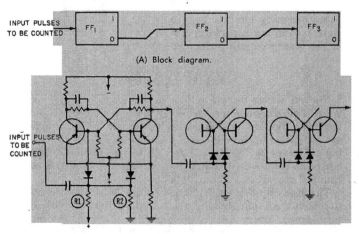

(A) Block diagram.

(B) Schematic.

Fig. 9-1. A simple binary counter.

2. The third row shows the second input-pulse applied. This complements FF_1 back to logical 0, triggering FF_2 to a logical-1 output, where the chain of output pulses stop. The binary total, 0010 equals decimal 2.
3. The fourth row shows the third input-pulse. This complements FF_1 to logical 1. However, FF_2 still has a logical-1 output, so a binary total of 0011 (decimal 3) is noted.
4. The fifth row shows the fourth pulse complementing FF_1 to logical 0. FF_1 provides a trigger output which comple-

128

ments FF_2 to logical 0. FF_2 provides a trigger output which complements FF_3 to logical 1 (binary 0100 or decimal 4).

With the 4-order counter shown, what is the highest decimal equivalent that can be counted? Go through the progressive steps, bit by bit, and prove the answer to be correct.

Of course this simple counter has limitations—especially in the matter of switching speed. With a multi-bit *word*, a serial type of counting operation might find this counter still switch-

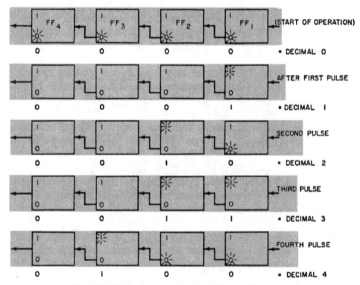

Fig. 9-2. Block diagram of single-bit counting.

ing through the higher-order elements of the first counting pulse as the next pulse is delivered. To prevent this possibility, parallel (rather than series) operation is frequently used.

Parallel Operation. In Fig. 9-3 is shown the schematic of the first flip-flop with its adjacent AND circuit. (This is the same electronic flip-flop circuit as was used in the previous circuit.) The AND circuit is enclosed by dashed lines. Remember, the signal comes in from the *right* in this schematic. The time lag normally present with series operation, with the attendant wait to present an indication of the new total, is substantially eliminated by using AND gates. With this arrangement, the input pulse is delivered to the lowest-order flip-flop (FF_1) and

129

all the conditioning inputs of the AND gates are applied simultaneously. Remember also that the AND circuit may operate on steady-state levels or pulses. Thus, these AND gates are already conditioned by the steady-state levels of their respec-

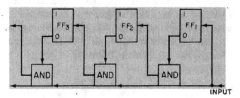

(A) Block diagram.

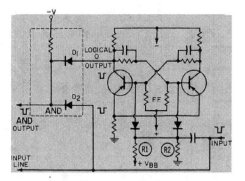

(B) Schematic of one stage.

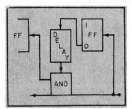

(C) Block diagram of one parallel stage with delay.

Fig. 9-3. Single-bit counting with parallel operation.

tive flip-flops, and require only the additional pulse to change each one *at the same time*, rather than serially. Therefore, if the flip-flops are all resting at their logical-0 outputs, the AND gates will be conditioned and will pass the input pulse without any transition time. As a result, the highest-order flip-flop would trip at the same time as the first one.

130

The AND circuit shown enclosed within the dashed lines is a simple diode configuration. The negative-going pulse would pass through D_2. Since $-V$ is sufficiently negative to be slightly below the lowest point expected of the pulse, except that D_1 is also conducting. The short-circuit that D_1 presents to the AND load resistance when logical-0 output is high, draws current through that resistor, causing a voltage-drop across it. As a result, the cathode of D_2 is not low enough for conduction. If, however, the output of the flip-flop is at a low logical-0 level, then it would present a more negative potential to D_1. This would reduce the voltage drop across the AND load resistance, so that the cathode end of D_2 is *conditioned* for receipt of the input pulse. Remember that the flip-flop and the AND gate are both part of a single-order counter element, and that the input pulse is applied to *every* AND gate at the same time. A similar electronic circuit would be found in each succeeding counter element (flip-flop-AND combination), providing parallel, and consequently, speedier counting.

There is one possible problem. The *same* input pulse which causes the flip-flop to provide a gate voltage to the AND circuit, may also pass through that AND circuit. This can occur if the input-pulse fall time is long in relation to the flip-flop gate-voltage rise time. This condition is undesirable because an extra count would be added to the flip-flop triggered by the AND circuit. To avoid this possibility, a simple delay circuit is inserted between the flip-flop and its related AND circuit, as shown by the boxed inset in Fig. 9-3. The delay can merely be a long co-axial cable, or one of the commercial passive time-delay electronic circuits. In either case, the switched signal from the flip-flop to the AND circuit is delayed until well after the initiating pulse has terminated.

Frequency Division. An interesting application in counting operations is the division-by-two action of flip-flops upon the frequency of the input signal. Since only one of the two possible outputs is generally used, and since that output is positive for one pulse and negative for the next, its waveform (in pulses) is only half that of the input signal. This is shown in the two-stage counter of Fig. 9-4. The schematic shows two identical flip-flops separated by a dashed line, distinguishing FF_1 from FF_2 in the equivalent logic diagram below. In this illustration the input signal comes from the left. Note the way the complementing action is shown in the logic diagram—with the input signal being applied to *both* the set and the reset inputs, causing simple complementary switching-action. The input frequency is 10 mc. This is stepped down at the output

131

of FF_1 to 5 mc which, in turn, is counted down to 2.5 mc at the output of FF_2.

The relationships of the waveforms involved are shown at the bottom of the diagram. Nothing happens at the outputs of FF_1 or FF_2 until the initiating pulse goes positive. The differentiating action of C_{C1} and R_{D1} provides a positive triggering pulse which passes through forward-bias S_{D2} (steering diode) to the base of the off-transistor X2, turning it on. This,

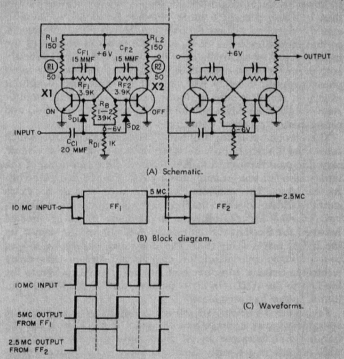

(A) Schematic.

(B) Block diagram.

(C) Waveforms.

Fig. 9-4. A two-stage counter.

of course, switches transistor X1 off. The load resistance of X1 is split between R1 and R_{L1} to standardize the circuit. (Consider R1 to be a stabilizing device which, even though cutting down the output slightly, makes the circuit more stable.) With X1 off, almost the entire +6 volts is available at the output. This is the rising waveform shown in the 5-mc output from FF_1 (lower portion of Fig. 9-4). This rising waveform has the same effect on FF_2 as the initiating positive-rising pulse did on FF_1, and causes a similar rising output. (Remember, the rapid pulse-repetition rate (PRR) makes the outputs of the flip-flops virtual pulses, rather than steady-state DC levels.)

The 10-mc input levels off at a maximum-positive potential, then starts down again to the lower level. The negative differentiated input-pulse resulting simply back-biases the steering diodes further, having no effect upon the counter. At this time the 10-mc input waveform starts moving positive again. This generates a positive differentiated spike, passing through S_{D1} (now forward-biased) since X1 is off. The input spike turns X1 on and X2 off (by flip-flop action). This causes a drop in the X1 output voltage which affects the 5-mc output from FF_1, as shown in the waveform. This negative-going output generates a negative differentiated spike in the input of FF_2, but this simply increases the back-bias on its steering diodes, so nothing happens to that flip-flop.

The 10-mc input levels off at a maximum-positive potential, then starts down again to the lower level. Continue the analysis to prove that the circuit in Fig. 9-4 is really a step-down counter.

In a practical application, the two-stage counter would have been preceded at the very beginning by a signal generator—any type that will develop the frequency desired—followed (just before the counter proper) by a Schmitt trigger circuit. The Schmitt trigger shapes the waveform in order to operate the counter with pulses rather than the sinewaves from the oscillator.

Schmitt Trigger

Although, generically speaking, the Schmitt trigger (Fig. 9-5) belongs to the flip-flop family, one is immediately taken by the omission of the familiar cross-coupling "X" seen in flip-flops. The reason for this is, one of the coupling networks is replaced by a common-emitter resistor. In the circuit shown, assume X1 to be on and X2 at cutoff with its collector voltage at −6 volts. This negative voltage is now the output.

A positive-going input signal enters through coupling capacitor C_1 to the base of X1, causing its collector voltage to change toward V_{CC} (from −2.5 to −6 volts). This is coupled through fast-coupling resistor-capacitor R_{F1}-C_{F1}, to the base of X2, changing its voltage from −0.4 to −6 volts. The increase in the base voltage of transistor X2 causes it to go from cutoff to conduction. This, in turn, causes the collector voltage of transistor X2 to change from −6 volts to approximately ground potential.

133

It is important, however, to note that this is *not a bistable* circuit resting in its new state. The moment the input signal drops to its quiescent reference-level, X1 base returns to its static point of −1.4 volts, permitting it to conduct. Static conditions are designed into the circuit to cut X2 off with no input signal. This is done with the voltage divider R_{B1} and R_{B2} between V_{CC} (−6 volts) and ground, and tapped at −1.4 volts for the X1 base. Since the common-emitter resistor R_E holds the emitter of X1 at −1 volt, X2 is cut off with no signal. Of course, when X2 is on, its heavy collector-current causes X1 to be cut off.

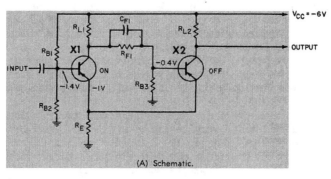

(A) Schematic.

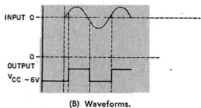

(B) Waveforms.

Fig. 9-5. A basic Schmitt trigger circuit.

The input waveforms in the diagram start at the zero reference line. The output, however, is down at −6 volts. When the input starts to rise, the output does too (after a slight circuit lag). Note, however, that the essentially sine-wave input has been nicely shaped to a square waveform for ideal counter operation. When the input waveform is passing through zero on its way to the negative peak, the output is still solidly switched to its most positive level (which is still below zero voltage reference). A moment later, with the input signal about half-way down to its negative peak, X1 is suddenly

134

turned on, causing the output to plunge to −6 volts. (Continue the analysis of the remainder of the waveform, referring to the schematic diagram for circuit action.) This slight delay before transistor X2 is switched off occurs because a slightly negative input is required to offset the higher emitter voltage caused by the collector current of transistor X2.

Fig. 9-6 shows the basic circuit modified to achieve a more sophisticated arrangement capable of operation from 100 cps to 10 mc. This modified circuit uses 2N695, 2N705, or 2N711

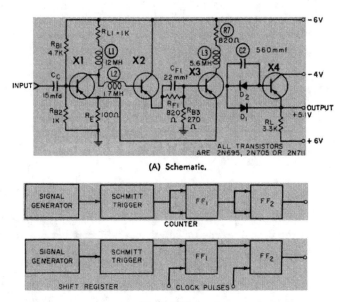

(A) Schematic.

(B) Block diagram.

Fig. 9-6. A 10-mc Schmitt trigger circuit.

mesa transistors (Fig. 9-6). Comparing this schematic diagram with the basic circuit, note that peaking coils L1, L2, and L3 have been inserted in the collector circuits to sharpen high-frequency response. Also, in conjunction with high-frequency response and circuit speed, the speed-up capacitor C_{F1} is relatively large for fast rise-time, but its resultant time constant must be small compared with the input pulse-repetition frequency. Therefore, the X3 (emitter follower) is inserted between C_{F1}-R_{F1} (speed-up network) to lower its impedance. Another fringe benefit in using the emitter follower is that

135

it provides a low-capacitance load to the collector of X1, further aiding in speeding up the switching action.

The output of the Schmitt trigger is taken from the collector of X2 through diode-capacitor input filter D2-C2, to the output emitter-follower X4 to provide a low-impedance output to drive the following counter. The emitter-follower output is developed across R_L, which provides a static reference of 5.1 volts. A silicon diode D1 is back-biased from the output back to the X2 collector. The diode acts as a fixed voltage drop so that the zero collector voltage of transistor X2 appears at the base of transistor X4 when transistor X2 is conducting. This offsets the voltage developed across emitter resistor R6.

The logic diagram below the schematic shows a block for a signal generator (any type) followed by the Schmitt trigger circuit (shown in the schematic), followed by a two-stage counter similar to the one described earlier in this chapter. The counter shown in Fig. 9-6, however, has one of the flip-flop inputs fed by clock pulses from an external source, slightly modifying the counter so that it now acts as a shift register. (The shift register operation is described in another topic later in this chapter.)

RING COUNTERS

When a counter is arranged so that a string of flip-flops connected in a closed loop move a single "bit" from any specified flip-flop to the next one when a single input-pulse is fed to all, the system is called a ring counter.

Assume a counter with three flip-flops in series, as shown in the upper logic diagram of Fig. 9-7. The indicator lights show the active state of the flip-flops before the input pulse is applied. Note that only one flip-flop (FF_2) has a logical 1 from a lower-order to a higher-order FF. Thus, it can be expected that as a result of an input pulse (applied from the right), the logical 1 will move from FF_2 to FF_3.

This input pulse is applied to all the zero inputs at the same time, and is so designed as to last only long enough for one flip-flop to switch states. (Of course, since the input pulse is applied to all the flip-flops at once, it will cause all the flip-flops to switch states if conditions are right for this to happen.) It is further specified that the logical-1 indicator is lighted when the logical-0 transistor conducts. (See the schematic of Fig. 9-7.) The on transistor is the logical-0 element of the flip-flop. The off transistor (logical-1 element) permits the logical-1 indicator (not shown) to light.

136

The input pulse is positive-going, which turns off the logical-0 transistor in FF_2, switching it and causing the logical-0 indicator to light. Meanwhile, the positive level developed in the logical-1 output of FF_2 turns the logical-1 transistor in FF_3 off, lighting the logical-1 indicator in FF_3. Since the logical-1 output of FF_3 is negative, it does not go on to switch FF_1. Of course, the input pulse was originally applied to the logical-0 inputs of FF_1 and FF_3 as well, but since these transistors were off at that time, no switching action took place.

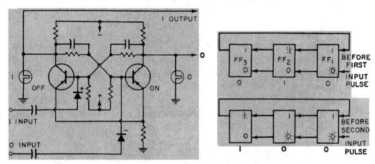

Fig. 9-7. A basic ring counter.

Look now at the lower logic diagram. Note that the logical-1 indicator in FF_3 is lighted. It is ready for the second input pulse. Remember that a lighted indicator in this circuit means its opposing input transistor is on. Thus, the positive input pulse now turns off the logical-0 input transistor of FF_3, causing its logical-0 indicator to light. The positive level out of the logical-1 transistor in FF_3 is coupled to the input of the logical-1 transistor of FF_1 turning it off, so the logical-1 indicator in FF_1 lights up. The output of the logical-1 transistor of FF_1 is now negative, so it does nothing to FF_2. The input pulse applied to the logical-0 inputs of FF_1 and FF_2 did nothing since these input transistors were off.

Note how the logical 1 has been moving from one flip-flop to the next higher one. Since there are only three flip-flops, they are looped around and started all over again. Some ring counters are not "closed," thus do not automatically proceed from the last device in the ring to the first one, but instead, other means are provided for turning off the first device. However, the closed-loop type of ring is quite popular, following generally the theory of operation described above. Where it is desired to speed up the action, AND circuits can be used, as is shown in the illustration of single-bit counting with par-

137

allel operation which was discussed in the previous chapter. Similarly, delay circuits can be introduced between the flip-flops to avoid switching chatter, or possibly false duplicate switching. This principle is shown in the same illustration in the previous chapter. The essence of the ring counter is the shifting of a bit *up* one place in a counting system. Where it is desired to shift a group of bits from one set of flip-flops to another for storage or for processing the data contained therein, the shift register is used.

SHIFT REGISTERS

The simple shift register shown in Fig. 9-8 serves to move the information in any vertical row of flip-flops (only one flip-flop is shown for each vertical row) to the next flip-flop to the right. The shift register is actually an open-loop ring counter in which more than one bit is inserted and shifted. Each flip-flop in this case has two input and two output lines.

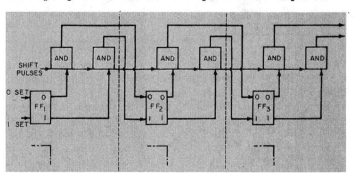

Fig. 9-8. A simple parallel shift-register.

Here, the inputs may be considered Set lines—that is, any input signal *sets* the logical figure marked for that line. Thus, a pulse applied to a Reset line (input) causes the flip-flop to switch to a logical-0 output if it was not already in that condition. (If it had been at logical-0 output, there would be no change.) The same action will occur if a pulse is applied to the Set line, except that the switching will cause a logical-1 output.

When it is desired to shift the reading in each flip-flop row (called a flip-flop register) to the next row on its right, a conditioning pulse (called a shift pulse) is applied to all the AND circuits simultaneously. (This action is also called *strobing* or

138

sensing the AND gates, inspecting them to see if they have information to pass on.) This shift pulse provides the second (coincident) input required to activate some of the AND gates (actually *half* of them in this case, since one out of every two must have the correct polarity to permit signal transfer when the shift pulse is applied), transferring (shifting) the signal intelligence from each register to the one adjacent.

A difficulty resulting from the arrangement shown may be that some of the flip-flops in one or more registers may receive new information from the previous register *before they can shift* their old information. This same sort of problem was solved before by inserting a delay in the input lines of the individual flip-flops, and the same method can be used in this case. The delay lines can even be inserted in the output. Actually, the delay lines serve as a sort of temporary storage device by their slowdown activity, so the information is not lost during the switching action that takes place as a result of the shifting activity.

REGISTER APPLICATIONS

The modern automatic washing machine is a clever device that will cycle itself through repeated water mixes, different motor speeds, change of operation from washing to rinsing to spin drying—even to turning itself off when finished! This has been programmed into the machine by a sequence generator which is usually a combination of mechanical and electrical components. In data-processing operations, it is also necessary sometimes to operate and to control devices in a sequential manner, so that the operation of a particular circuit has a fixed relationship to all other circuit functions, either in time relationship, or in sequence operation. The circuits discussed up to this point can be assembled to produce such a sequence generator.

The Sequence Generator

The logic circuit of a sequence generator is shown in Fig. 9-9. The incoming clock pulses have been previously set up (as explained earlier in the book) to control the switching rate and to allow full synchronization of these circuits with other circuit functions. The three-stage binary counter is used to *count* (step down) the input clock-pulses and to utilize the resultant output in binary form. The diode AND-gates act as binary-count sensors, converting different arrangements of counter outputs into decimal equivalents. Since only three

139

counter stages are used for the basic sequence generator, there are only eight possible combinations of output states. As a result, there will only be eight sequence pulses. A fourth counter would permit going beyond eight—but then, it is unknown which decimal count will be required for the ultimate

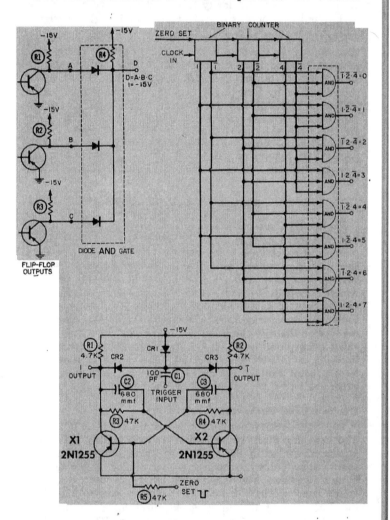

Fig. 9-9. A basic sequence generator.

data-processing operation. The important advantage of this type of sequence control is that the switching rate is controlled solely by the input clock-pulses, which may be adjusted from a very slow rate up to the maximum frequency at which the binary counter is capable of operating. Analyzing the logical operation of the basic block diagram, it is found that each of the three flip-flops operating as binary counters has two outputs. These outputs have previously been called F and $\bar{F}$ or logical 1 and logical 0. Here, the outputs of the first flip-flop will be given the digital values 1 and $\bar{1}$, the outputs of the second flip-flop 2 and $\bar{2}$, and the outputs of the third flip-flop 4 and $\bar{4}$. So long as numerical values are assigned to the outputs, and are related properly and consistently, the arithmetic will not suffer. (It may help to think of the counters in reverse order. The first one on the right is the lowest-order binary place, with the binary values increasing toward the left. Also think of the outputs as binary 1 and 0. The first unit represents 2^0, the next unit being 2^1, and the third being 2^2. It may also help to consider the assigned output values as though each is lighting a corresponding output lamp with the digital value illuminated.)

Now examine the uppermost AND gate. The three coincident inputs that would operate that gate are $\bar{1}, \bar{2}, \bar{4}$. When these are ANDed together, they total *not anything*, or 0 as shown. Remember, the AND gates are being used to convert from binary notation (machine notation) to decimal counting (human notation). The second AND gate operates upon coincidence of inputs $1, \bar{2}, \bar{4}$, which represents a decimal value of 1. Similarly, the gates below add up the equivalent decimal values assigned to the bits and provide a gate output of the decimal total. Thus the bottom AND gate, showing a coincident input of 1, 2, 4, provides an output level designated as decimal 7.

The electronic equivalent of the preceding paragraph can be worked out with the schematic of the diode AND-gate shown in Fig. 9-9. If all three transistors are off, their outputs will all show −15 volts. Since very little current now will be flowing through R4 the diodes are reverse-biased, the output at D will be the power-supply voltage of −15 volts. The output can be considered a logical 1, or any other logical meaning that has been assigned to the significant output of this particular AND circuit. If any one (or more) of the transistors is on, the AND-circuit output voltage (at A, B, or C) will rise to a more positive value. Current will pass through the respective diode, raising the voltage at the bottom of R4 to a more positive value. This will produce an output of logical 0 or whatever has been assigned to this AND gate as *other* than the *significant output* desired.

The electronic circuitry of the saturated-mode binary flip-flop with counter input is also shown in Fig. 9-9. What is especially significant in this circuit is not the *1* and *1̄* output, since these have been discussed before as logical-*1* and logical-*0* outputs, but rather the input to the X1 base through series input-resistor R5. This input is designated as Zero Set (called Reset, or Set logical *0* before). This input is shown as a common strobing pulse in the basic block diagram and as the Trigger Input applied through coupling capacitor C1, in the schematic diagram. The positive trigger passes through CR2 or CR3, whichever is forward-biased at the time, to deliver a

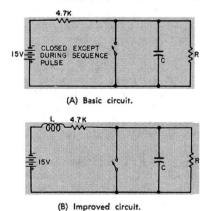

(A) Basic circuit.

(B) Improved circuit.

Fig. 9-10. Equivalent circuit for one basic sequence-generator output.

positive pulse to the respective collector and turn the on transistor off, switching the circuit. The Zero-Set input is applied to all counters at the beginning of the operations, *clearing the counters* and thus permitting this phase of the operation to be synchronized with all other functions. The equivalent circuit for the sequence-generator output of one of these *conditioning* pulses is shown in Fig. 9-10A. Any capacity in the load tends to slow up the rise and fall time of the output pulse. Thus, when the basic circuit switch is opened, the circuit capacity degrades the waveform really meant for load resistor R. To compensate for the inherent circuit capacitance, an inductor (L) is inserted in series with the input resistor, as shown in Fig. 9-10B.

142

The inductance value (5 mh) is not critical. Any circuit ringing or waveform overshoot that might occur if L is too large will be clamped by one of the counters. Rather than place a coil in each leg of the sequence generator, only two are used— one in the "even" and one in the "odd" leg as shown in Fig. 9-11.

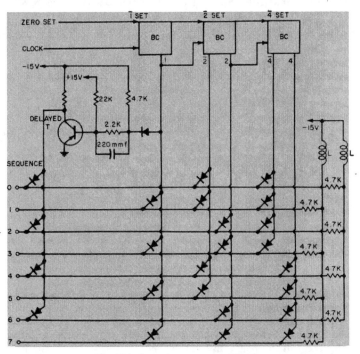

Fig. 9-11. Sequence-generator schematic.

It might be said that whatever the ultimate function of any sequence generator, the first stage in the counter involved will have to operate at least as fast as any other stage. At any given instant, no matter what information has gone before, every clock pulse will trigger the first counter stage (whether or not it triggers any other). So the first and second counter stages (at least) usually have provision for minimum delay. The possible difficulty arising from trigger delays in these stages is shown by the waveforms in Fig. 9-12A. The top line shows a series of positive clock-pulses of such short duration that they seem to have no width at all. In an earlier paragraph

143

(see Fig. 9-4) count-down operation was explained. Accordingly, the $\bar{1}$ output shows four output pulses for the eight received. Similarly, the $\bar{2}$ output shows two output pulses and the $\bar{4}$ output shows only one. Referring back to Fig. 9-9, note that the output of the uppermost AND gate shows $\bar{1} \cdot \bar{2} \cdot \bar{4} = 0$. This provides the sequence-0 output. Now, back again to Fig. 9-12A, note that the sequence 0 pulse contains two negative spikes A and B (greatly exaggerated for clarity) in addition to the desired broad positive pulse. (This is the ANDed version

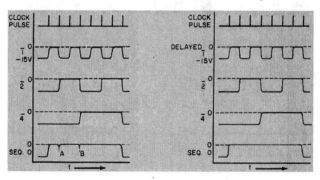

(A) With trigger delays in
the binary counter.

(B) Inverter circuit added.

Fig. 9-12. Sequence-generator waveforms.

of the three waveforms above it.) The spike at A is caused by the undesired coincidence of the $\bar{1}$ and $\bar{2}$ pulses due to the finite fall and rise times. Upon the arrival of the second clock-pulse, the first binary-counter stage is reset from its original positive output at $\bar{1}$ to a negative output voltage at $\bar{1}$. Because of the slight delay in the triggering of the second counter-stage, the $\bar{2}$ voltage is not decayed when the $\bar{1}$ is applied, thus introducing a spike.

In a similar manner, a spike is produced at point B due to the undesired coincidence of the $\bar{2}$ and $\bar{4}$ pulses caused by the finite switching times. (In practice, this spike at B is usually smaller than the spike at A because of the lesser delay.)

As a solution to the problem, an inverter stage consisting of a type 2N1255 double-diffused transistor is added, as shown in Fig. 9-11, to supply the $\bar{1}$ pulse. The output of the inverter is a $\bar{1}$ signal which remains at zero voltage for a time slightly longer than the $\bar{1}$ pulse obtained directly from the binary-counter stage. The transistor is very heavily driven into satu-

144

ration, thus giving a fast turn-on with a fairly long storage time. This transistor can be considered a part of the first BC, since it is diode-coupled to the logical-*1* output, and as such, is part of the first boxed enclosure.

The pulse conditions with the inverter circuit added may be seen in Fig. 9-12B. The time delays have again been exaggerated for clarity. Note, however, that the waveform of *sequence 0* is now *clean.*

The schematic in Fig. 9-11 is really a combination schematic-logic diagram, showing the binary counters (BC) as logic blocks, with the delayed-*1* inverter and the AND gates in schematic form. Each BC-logic block can be replaced with the "Binary Flip-Flop with Counter Input" schematic shown in Fig. 9-9. The earnest reader is encouraged to draw a large schematic of the entire sequence generator showing all values of all components, trace out all circuitry, and be able to explain the function of every component. This will provide an excellent self-checking device on comprehension of the material supplied to this point.

Once that is done, work out the signal paths and circuit activity resulting from all possible combinations of inputs. First consider the effect of a Zero-Set pulse applied from an external source. Then, consider the response of eight clock pulses (one at a time) as shown in Fig. 9-12B. Finally, trace the eight possible decimal values under *SEQUENCE* in the schematic shown in Fig. 9-11.

REVIEW QUESTIONS

1. How does a binary counter work?

2. What is the disadvantage of a series binary counter?

3. How is this disadvantage overcome?

4. How does a flip-flop perform frequency division?

5. What is one application of the Schmitt trigger?

6. How does a Schmitt trigger work?

7. How does a ring counter work?

CHAPTER 10

Tunnel Diodes

The tunnel diode is a high-frequency switching device having a great potential as a component for ultra high-speed digital computers. In addition, it has bi-stable properties which make it useable as a storage element similar to the flip-flop and magnetic core.

BASIC THEORY

The volt-ampere characteristic curve of the tunnel diode (Fig. 10-1) shows an area of operation in which increasing the forward voltage causes a decreasing value of forward current. This portion of the characteristics curve is said to represent negative resistance. That is, the slope is negative as opposed to the positive slope for conventional resistance.

This negative-resistance property of the tunnel diode makes it useful as a switching device. Note that the conditions at the peak and valley point are similar to those of a closed and an open switch. The peak current (about 3 milliamperes in some cases) occurs at a low forward-voltage in a manner similar to a closed switch or a saturated transistor. The point of minimum current (about 1 milliampere in some cases), is associated with a higher forward-voltage just as the high voltage across an open switch or cut-off transistor is accompanied by a low current.

Switching Characteristics

The tunnel diode is made to switch between two stable states as a result of a load resistor and input current (Fig. 10-2). Thus the circuit is similar to a flip-flop or a toggle switch.

The value of the load resistance connected in series between the plate of the tunnel diode and the power supply is selected to provide a current less than the peak current. This results in an output voltage of approximately 0.01 volts (operating

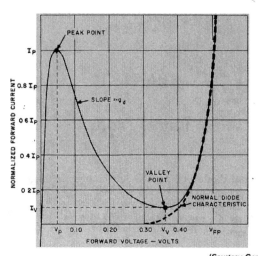

(Courtesy General Electric)

Fig. 10-1. Static characteristics of a typical germanium tunnel diode.

point a). When left untriggered, the circuit stays in this state indefinitely.

Turn-On. The application of a very narrow positive turn-on voltage-pulse at the input causes the voltage and current of the tunnel diode to increase until the peak-current point is reached. Beyond this peak-current point, the circuit switches

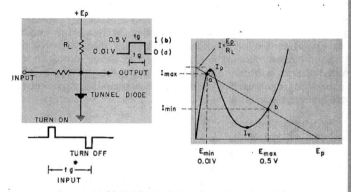

*TYPICAL $t_g = 10^{-9}$ SECONDS = 1 NANOSECOND = 1 MILLIMICROSECOND

Fig. 10-2. A tunnel-diode bistable switch.

148

to operating point b as soon as the turn-on pulse is removed. Circuit switching is caused by the current-limiting properties of the load resistor since the tunnel-diode voltage is a function of the same series current. The current through the load resistor is directly related to the *difference* between the supply voltage and the voltage across the tunnel diode.

At the peak-current point, the voltage across the tunnel diode is greater than it was at point a. This means that the voltage *difference* across the load resistor is less, and hence will result in a smaller series-current flow. The smaller current flow through the tunnel diode results in greater voltage being developed across it.

The greater voltage across the tunnel diode results in smaller current flow through the resistor. This causes an even greater voltage across the tunnel diode. As can be seen, this process will continue until less series-current flow *does not* result in a higher voltage across the tunnel diode. This process (called regeneration or positive feedback) ceases when the valley point is reached.

At the valley point, however, the sum of the voltage drop across the tunnel diode and the drop across the load resistor is less than the supply voltage. This causes the voltage across the tunnel diode to increase, and consequently, an increased current to flow through it. This process results in the voltage and current values at operating point b.

At operating point b, the sum of the voltage drops across the tunnel diode and the load resistor equal the supply voltage. Thus, point b becomes the stable operating-point after switching. The circuit will remain in this state until a turn-off pulse is applied.

Turn-Off. A very narrow negative turn-off voltage-pulse is applied to the input. The turn-off pulse causes current flow through the load resistor which reduces the tunnel-diode plate voltage. When this plate voltage is reduced below the valley-point voltage, the circuit switches back to stable-state a.

The switch-back occurs because the currents to the left of the valley-point voltage create voltage drops across the load resistor which lowers the tunnel-diode voltage even more. As this voltage is lowered, higher currents flow, causing the tunnel-diode voltage to be reduced even further. This process continues until the peak current is reached.

Past the peak-current point, the tunnel-diode voltage reduces as a result of the voltage drop across the load resistor, and the current is also reduced. This continues until operating point a is reached.

ANALOG-THRESHOLD TUNNEL-DIODE LOGIC

It has been noted earlier that a tunnel diode will switch from the low-voltage, high-current state (point *a*) to the high-voltage, low-current state (point *b*) when peak current is drawn. When combinations of input voltages are used to supply this peak current, logic functions can be performed. For example, if *either* of two inputs can supply peak current to the tunnel-diode circuit, the OR function is performed. That is, one or the other input can switch the diode.

On the other hand, if two input voltages must be simultaneously present in order to cause peak-current flow, the AND function is performed. Since this mode of operation is similar to analog addition by current summing, the arrangement is called analog logic. When the threshold (peak or valley current) is reached, these circuits switch.

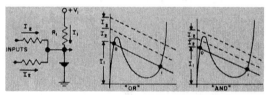

(Courtesy General Electric)

Fig. 10-3. Tunnel-diode threshold logic.

The tunnel-diode OR and AND circuit (Fig. 10-3) have the same configuration. The input resistance values, however, are different. In the case of the OR circuit, the load line created by the input resistance and voltage pulse at either input, will cause peak current to flow. In the case of the AND circuit, however, input pulses must be simultaneously present at both inputs before peak tunnel-diode current will be drawn. Note that, in either case, a separate input (not shown) is required for turn-off.

Analog-threshold tunnel-diode logic does, however, have a few limitations. The most severe is the fact that there is no signal isolation between stages. That is, the input signals applied to the plate are also coupled to the following stage and, conversely, voltages developed across the next stage are coupled back to the tunnel diode. As a result of this isolation problem and false triggering possibilities, other tunnel-diode logic circuits have been developed.

150

Goto-Pair Tunnel-Diode Majority Logic Circuits

GOTO-pair circuits (named after E. Goto, the Japanese scientist who first proposed this circuit arrangement) will isolate stages and reduce circuit variations. The basic element of Goto-pair logic consists of two tunnel diodes connected in series (Fig. 10-4). These tunnel diodes, called a "twin" circuit because they have almost identical characteristics, are periodically actuated by clock pulses, at which time one of the two tunnel diodes will always switch to the high-voltage low-

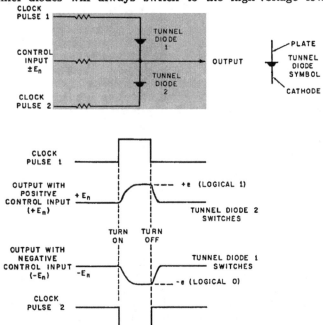

Fig. 10-4. A Goto-pair circuit.

current state. When one of the diodes switch, the voltage across the other diode is insufficient to cause it to switch. As a result, only one of the pair can be switched to the high-voltage low-current state at one time.

A control voltage is used to select which one of the two is to be switched. A positive control-voltage puts diode 2 in the proper condition while a negative control-voltage will condition diode 1. The actual switching, however, will occur only upon application of the clock pulses. These clock pulses act as

151

power supplies for the diodes and are turned on and off as many as 30 million times a second (30 mc).

The control voltage causes a small additional current to flow through one or the other of the tunnel diodes. This additional current causes the associated diode to switch when the clock pulses are applied. Since the tunnel diodes are polarity sensitive, a positive control-voltage makes the plate of tunnel diode 2 more positive, causing additional current flow in that diode. Conversely, a negative control-voltage makes the cathode of tunnel diode 1 more negative, causing additional current flow in that unit.

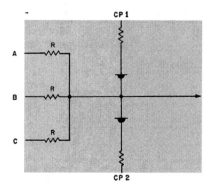

Fig. 10-5. A Goto-pair MAJORITY circuit.

Majority-Control Inputs. Consider the case of a Goto pair (twin circuit) having more than one control input (Fig. 10-5). In practice, all input voltages have one of two standard values. Logical *1* is represented by a pulse which is positive by a few volts and logical *0* by a pulse which is negative by a few volts.

The choice of resistance values makes the majority circuit perform either the AND, OR, or the MAJORITY function. The MAJORITY function consists of responding to the logical state represented by the majority of the inputs. This function is performed when *each* input resistance will pass enough current to switch the tunnel-diode pair. If one of the three inputs is logical *0* and another is logical *1*, however, the currents will cancel. That is, one input voltage will draw all the current supplied by the other. Since the two opposite inputs cancel each other, the circuit response will be determined by the third input. When the third input is logical *1*, the circuit will switch

152

to the logical-*1* state. When the third input is logical-*0* it will switch to the logical-*0* state.

In any case, a simple majority of inputs (at least two out of three) must be present before the circuit will switch to the state represented by that majority. This function is useful in selection and control circuits which must be governed by the larger number of digital quantities or conditions. For example, the parity checking of parallel bits in computer words could be accomplished using the majority function.

The AND function is performed by majority logic when the resistance values require that all inputs must be logical 1, before sufficient switching current is available. By the same token, the resistance values can be selected so that any logical-*1* input voltage provides sufficient switching current. This results in an OR function.

Phase-Locked Operation. In the discussion of Goto-pair logic it was said that this mode of operation provided isolation and freedom from variations in tunnel-diode characteristics due to temperature effects. This is accomplished through the use of phase-locked operation. The problem of interaction between stages is solved by a rather unique method. Instead of carrying out all switching and logic operations at the same time, three sets of different non-coincident, but over-lapping, clock pulses are used. In other words, if three logic stages operate in cascade, each stage is made to turn on at a different time. As a result, undesired transient signals coupled between stages during turn-on do not affect the other stages since the other stages are not turned on at that time.

This arrangement is called phase-locked operation because each stage is gated on by (locked to) clock pulses which are out of phase with each other. In addition, characteristics changes due to temperature variations are reduced because the circuit is pulse operated. Thus, the circuits are not heated by DC-power dissipation since they are not continuously operated. This also reduces the ambient temperature of the equipment. The power dissipated as a result of the pulsed operation is fairly low because the clock pulses can be made very short in relation to their repetition frequency.

The phased clock-pulses (Fig. 10-6) only determine when the tunnel-diode stages will operate. The logic inputs determine the logical output of a stage. Note, however, that the logical output of a phase-locked stage occurs only for the duration of the clock pulse applied to it. As a result, the phase of the logic input in relation to the phase of the timing input becomes an important consideration. For example, suppose the

153

logic inputs to stage 3 were in phase with phase-1 clock pulses. Since the stage is operated by phase-3 clock pulses, the logic inputs would never be present when stage 3 was gated on by the timing input. Conversely, the logic inputs would be applied to the stage when it was cut off.

Also note that the effects of input voltages can be coupled from one stage to another. Because of the high series resistances, however, the input voltage at one stage will usually not affect a tunnel-diode circuit two stages away. This also applies

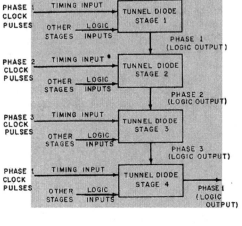

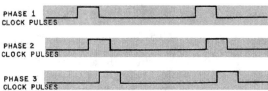

Fig. 10-6. Phase-locked tunnel-diode operation.

to the voltages fed back from one tunnel-diode stage to the preceding one. Thus, if the stages before and after a gated tunnel-diode stage are operated out of phase with it, it does not matter if circuits two stages way from the gated stage are also gated. This is why only three different clock phases are required. For example, in Fig. 10-6, stages 1 and 4 are both operated by phase-1 clock pulses. This means that stage 4 is gated on at the same time as stage 1. Because of the coupling attenuation between stages, however, transients from these two stages do not interact.

154

To sum up, the basic Goto-pair tunnel-diode stage (Fig. 10-7) consists of both a clock-pulse and a logic input circuit. The clock-pulse input circuit transforms the input clock-pulses into two 180 degree out-of-phase (see Fig. 10-4) pulses. The logic input, however, determines which diode is to switch.

In addition to phase-locked operation, other isolation techniques are sometimes used. Conventional diodes and transistors can be used in conjunction with the tunnel diodes to

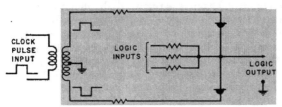

Fig. 10-7. A complete Goto-pair tunnel-diode stage.

provide stage-to-stage isolation. However, when these conventional diodes and transistors are used, the overall switching speeds are generally reduced, introducing a limitation not present in phase-locked systems.

TUNNEL DIODE FLIP-FLOPS

A tunnel-diode circuit (Fig. 10-8) can be constructed that will perform binary counting and other flip-flop functions. In the circuit shown, the value of a common load-resistor is selected so that only one diode can be in the high-current low-

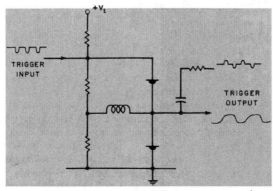

Fig. 10-8. A basic tunnel-diode flip-flop circuit.

voltage state at a time. The current flowing through the inductor is supplied by whichever of the diodes is in this high-current state.

The application of a negative trigger-pulse causes the voltage across both diodes to become negative. This causes the unit which was in the high-voltage low-current state to be switched back to the low-voltage high-current state for as long as the trigger pulse is present.

When the trigger pulse is removed, the induced voltage in the inductor switches the diodes. That is, the inductor causes a current flow that switches the diode which was originally in the high-current condition to the low-current high-voltage state. Since the circuit output is taken from between the plate of the lower tunnel diode and ground, the output will represent the state of the lower tunnel diode.

REVIEW QUESTIONS

1. What is negative resistance?

2. How is a negative-resistance device used as a switching circuit?

3. What particular advantage do tunnel diodes provide?

4. What is the operating principle of Analog-threshold logic?

5. What is the principle of the Goto pair?

6. What are some tunnel diode limitations that must be compensated for?

7. How are these limitations compensated for?

8. What is phase-locked operation?

CHAPTER 11

Transistor-Driven Magnetic Cores

Transistors are often used to provide the current pulses needed to drive magnetic-core logic circuits. The basic transistor and core combination provides a low-power, compact, and flexible logic element.

MAGNETIC CORE CHARACTERISTICS

The magnetic cores used for logic operations are constructed of high-retentivity magnetic material. The direction of current flowing through the windings determines the direction of magnetic flux within the core. The high retentivity of the magnetic material causes much of this flux to remain *even after the magnetizing current has been removed*. In this manner, the direction of the magnetic flux in a core is used to store binary and logical 1's and 0's.

The direction of magnetic flux, and hence the logical state of the core, is indicated in terms of voltages induced in a pick-up winding. (See Fig. 11-1.) The core is driven by current pulses which switch the flux direction. One flux direction is considered as the logical-1 condition and the other logical 0.

The use of magnetic cores is similar to the use of flip-flops. The core is initially reset to the logical-0 state ($-\phi1$) by passing a current of $-I1$ through the reset winding. The behavior of the core now depends upon the condition of the Set input. A positive current pulse ($+I1$) applied to the Set input causes the flux direction to switch to the logical-1 state ($+\phi1$). This causes the magnetic field to change, inducing a voltage in the pick-up coil. This voltage is not desired at this time and is blocked by the crystal diode.

The next Reset pulse ($-I1$) switches the core back to the logical-0 state ($-\phi1$). The changing flux associated with the switch from $+\phi1$ to $-\phi1$ induces a voltage in the pick-up loop. This voltage is opposite in polarity to that caused by the Set pulse and, therefore, forward biases the diode causing current flow in the output load. In this manner the magnetic core indicates that a Set input was applied and stored by the flux direction of the core.

It is important to note that the core does not provide an output voltage except during Reset. Moreover, this output voltage can only occur after the flux direction in the core has been switched to the logical-*1* state ($+\phi 1$) by a previous Set input.

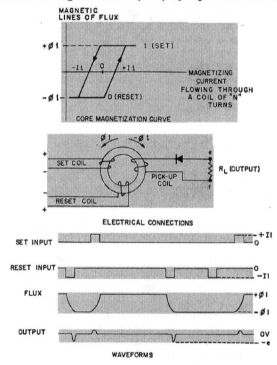

Fig. 11-1. Magnetic-core characteristics.

TRANSISTOR DRIVERS

In the discussion of the magnetic core, current pulses were mentioned as the means of driving. These current pulses are developed by driver circuits (Fig. 11-2) which act like a switch. When the driver conducts, current flows through the core windings and switches the direction of the flux. The direction of current flow through the winding, and hence the

158

direction of the flux set up by this current, is determined by the connections to the coils.

Small input currents operate the driver transistors, which, in turn, provide the higher currents used to switch the cores. As a result, the Set and Reset input-pulses do not have to supply the actual switching current. This allows a relatively small current to operate the drivers of a number of magnetic cores.

A dot is used to identify coil terminals. Current flowing into the input terminal with the dot will create a magnetic flux in one direction, while currents flowing into the other terminal (without the dot) cause a magnetic flux in the other direction.

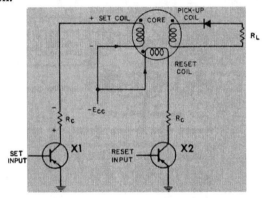

Fig. 11-2. A basic transistor-driven magnetic-core circuit.

In the case of voltages, the dot indicates polarity. All terminals with a dot will have the same instantaneous polarity as that applied to the dot terminal on the driver coil. For example, when transistor X1 conducts, the collector current will cause the dot terminal of the Set coil to be positive. The voltages induced in the other coils by the changing magnetic flux will cause the terminals with a dot to also be positive.

In practice, a single transistor is used to drive more than one core (Fig. 11-3). It provides the current to Reset its associated core and also to Set the next core. In the circuit shown, the transistor driver conducts only when core 1 goes from the logical-1 flux direction to the logical-0 flux direction. Circuit operation is very similar to that of a blocking oscillator. The transistor driver is normally held cutoff by the negative bias applied to the emitter. However, when the core has been previously Set to logical 1, the Reset trigger-pulse causes a changing flux in the magnetic core.

159

This changing flux induces a negative voltage in the driver input-coil, causing base current to flow in the transistor driver. This base current, in turn, causes a collector current to flow through the Reset drive-coil, causing additional changing magnetic flux in the core. As a result, the greater induced voltage in the driver input-coil causes more base current and greater collector-current flow. The increasing collector current, in turn, induces a larger voltage in the driver input-coil.

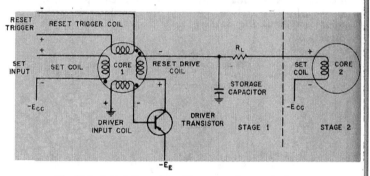

Fig. 11-3. A typical transistor-driven magnetic-core circuit.

This process of positive feedback continues to build up until the core is switched from logical 1 ($+\phi1$) to logical 0 ($-\phi1$). At that time, additional collector current will no longer produce a changing magnetic flux. Consequently, no voltage is induced in the driver input-coil and the transistor returns to cutoff.

When the core flux is in the logical-0 direction at the time a Reset trigger is applied, nothing happens. The Reset trigger creates a flux in the logical-0 direction, and since the core flux is *already* in that direction, no changing flux is created. Consequently, there is no negative voltage induced in the driver input-coil, and the transistor remains cutoff.

Note that the same collector current used to reset core 1 also sets core 2. Since the collector current flows only when core 1 is reset from the logical-1 state, core 2 is only set to logical-1 when core 1 has previously been in that state.

The storage capacitor introduces a long rise time for the set current to core 2. As a result, core 2 is set slightly after core 1 is reset. This delay is necessary so that the set and reset operation do not occur at the same instant. This would be highly undesirable because it would result in unpredictable operation. That is, it would be impossible to tell whether the core would

160

remain set or would become reset under these conditions. Thus, the storage capacitor ensures that the following core will not be set until it's previous state is returned to logical *0* (reset). A phase-locked reset system is sometimes used to cause the delay (see phase-locked operation in Chapter 11).

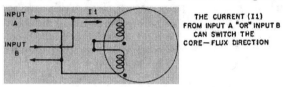

THE CURRENT (I1) FROM INPUT A "OR" INPUT B CAN SWITCH THE CORE—FLUX DIRECTION

(A) The OR function.

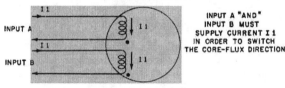

INPUT A "AND" INPUT B MUST SUPPLY CURRENT I 1 IN ORDER TO SWITCH THE CORE-FLUX DIRECTION

(B) The AND function.

Fig. 11-4. Logical operations using magnetic cores.

LOGICAL OPERATIONS

Now that the operation of a core with a single input winding is understood it will be easier to visualize how these cores are used to perform the AND and OR function.

When a magnetic core is connected so that any one of two (or more) inputs will supply the required flux-direction switching current, the logical OR function is performed (Fig. 11-4A). With proper internal connections the circuit can be arranged so that individual current inputs are not capable of switching the core. In this case, *both* current inputs must be present in order to accomplish the switching operation. As a result, the logical AND function is performed (Fig. 11-4B). Both are required to switch the core because each input current flows only through half of the total number of coil turns. Stated another way, each current input supplies only half of the ampere-turns required, so both must be present in order to switch the core.

MAGNETIC-CORE COMPUTER SYSTEMS

It is possible to use transistor-driven magnetic cores to perform complete computer operations. Magnetic-core circuits can be used to count, do logic operations, perform control operations, store data, and perform arithmetic operations. Moreover, most of these operations can be performed using a single general-purpose circuit.

General-Purpose Circuits

A typical general-purpose circuit (Fig. 11-5) can be connected in many different ways to provide many different functions. Note that the basic circuit contains a dual set-coil (see Fig. 11-4) discussed previously. Also note that the circuit is identical to that shown in Fig. 11-3.

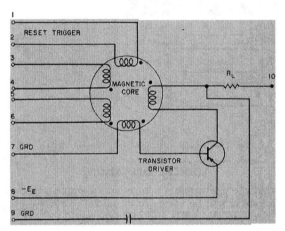

Fig. 11-5. A typical general-purpose transistor-driven magnetic-core logic circuit.

The basic magnetic-core system consists of an oscillator to supply reset trigger-pulses, power supplies for the driver transistors, and data-input devices such as punched-card readers, toggle switches, analog-to-digital converters, and other digital data-processing equipment.

REVIEW QUESTIONS

1. How are transistors used with magnetic cores?
2. How are magnetic cores used to store data?
3. How are magnetic cores used to perform the AND and OR functions?
4. Why are general-purpose transistor–driven magnetic-core modules used?
5. What type of circuit does the general-purpose module resemble?

162

CHAPTER 12

Packaging and Mechanization

Any computer is composed of certain components which make up circuits. These circuits, in turn, provide functions of increasing complexity, making up the entire computer. Although the electrical function may be the same, many different mechanical arrangements could be used to do the same job. The arrangement of chassis in the cabinet could be different. The selection of logical blocks making up the circuits could be different. The mechanical layout and the way the machine is put together constitute its packaging.

PACKAGING

Packaging a variety of fundamental components and their circuits are shown in Fig. 12-1. The conventional metal chassis of the type used in the majority of electronic equipment, circa 1920 through 1960, is seen in Fig. 12-1A. On these metal chassis were mounted boxes, cans, and brackets housing the major components, while beneath were additional small components and wiring. Sockets atop the chassis accommodated vacuum tubes.

With the advent of computers with their somewhat repetitious logic circuitry, new packaging concepts were suggested. This led to the long, narrow strip unit as in Fig. 12-1B with components mounted on top and wiring beneath. Certain television receivers still use this "IF-strip" construction as a subassembly. A vertical-strip mounting which better utilizes the space in certain applications is seen in Fig. 12-1C, while in Fig. 12-1D is shown an angled construction, again mechanically fitting the circuitry to the equipment package. Finally, Fig. 12-1E shows a completely flat circuit board upon which circuit lines are printed and upon which is mounted the individual components.

All these varieties illustrate only a very small range of packaging concepts involved in computer design.

Modular Concept

Practically any computer may be expressed as a collection of AND, OR, and similar simple logic blocks. Thus, under a mass production program, a computer manufacturer finds it economical to start an assembly line going. For example, AND circuits in a small, individual logic package may be produced

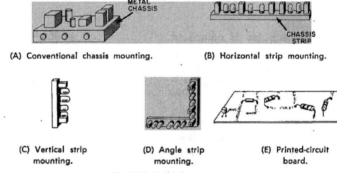

(A) Conventional chassis mounting.   (B) Horizontal strip mounting.

(C) Vertical strip mounting.   (D) Angle strip mounting.   (E) Printed-circuit board.

Fig. 12-1. Packaging concepts.

on this line. Whenever an order for a computer is received, large numbers of these small logic packages are available which can be connected (or plugged in) to make up the large machine. This very simply expresses the modular concept.

Figure 12-2 shows one example of this concept. The very basic logic circuit is packaged in its own module, which in the example shown, is a cylinder similar to a vacuum tube. This module, with many of its identical brothers, is plugged into a rack having intersocket wiring. This entire rack then becomes a logic register able to perform a function much more complex than any of the individual logic modules. A number of these logic registers are then interconnected on a larger frame making up an entire operational element such as the arithmetic unit of the computer.

Of course the modular concept can be modified to use printed-circuit wiring. It may even use thin-film circuits. This latter type has the inter-circuit wiring deposited onto the insulating chassis by a vaporizing process taking place in a vacuum chamber. The important thing to understand is, however, that the modular concept permits manufacture of iden-

164

tical and smaller packages using mass-production techniques. This effects economy, uniformity, and ultimately, improved reliability.

Reliability of Packaging

In many computer applications (especially those concerned with strategic military operations) the reliability of the machine must be as nearly perfect as possible. Under certain conditions, production cost is virtually ignored in an attempt to achieve maximum reliability. Some designers use twice as many components as are necessary to perform a circuit function, virtually paralleling all elements. They do this so that if one component fails, its parallel twin will continue to operate. This, appropriately enough, is called, *component redundancy*.

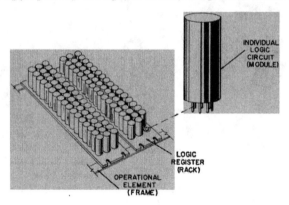

Fig. 12-2. Modular packaging.

It does, in some cases, provide improved reliability. (It might be argued that more components provide more opportunity for component failure . . . and that is correct. Just the same, redundancy is an approved circuit design technique.) This is where packaging contributes a great deal to computer design. It permits mass production of practically identical modular units, both for redundancy in construction, and for stock replacement in case of failure.

Printed-Circuit Boards

Already popular in table-model radio receivers and in television sets, the printed-circuit board (Fig. 12-3) has proved itself in computer applications as a lightweight, efficient, low-cost circuit "chassis." Note that the individual circuit boards

165

are phenolic or fibre insulating sheets, upon which the conventional components are mounted by means of holes in the card which permit the pig-tail leads to be pushed in place. Metallic connecting lines are laid on the boards, either by metallic paint or by an etching process. These "printed" circuit lines connect the components. The different boards are at-

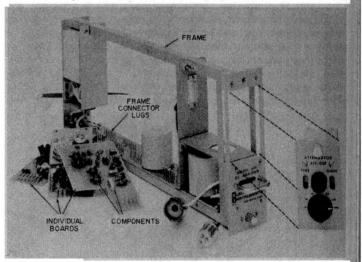

(Courtesy Electro Instruments, Inc.)

Fig. 12-3. Printed-circuit boards and mounting frame.

tached to the skeleton-like frame, with connections made to the wiring lugs.

The assembled unit is shown in Fig. 12-4. Note the extended lugs attached to the printed circuit lines. A conventional wire connects these lugs to the frame lugs, completing the connections. When any particular circuit is believed to be faulty, a few machine screws free the particular board, the frame connections are unsoldered, and it can be removed for ready replacement with a spare kept for this purpose. (The faulty board can be tested and repaired at leisure, without contributing to computer "down time.")

The accessibility of the components on the printed boards makes it possible to service the circuits in the conventional manner if no replacement is available. Note that the frame forms a "drawer" which can fit into a cabinet opening. The connectors at the back of the frame make electrical connection for each printed-circuit board through the frame connector lugs

166

END FRAME CONNECTORS
DRAWER

(Courtesy Electro Instruments, Inc.)

Fig. 12-4. Printed-circuit boards assembled in frame.

to the cabinet wiring, completing the inter-drawer wiring for the entire system.

Modules

As printed-circuit boards became more popular, astute computer designers realized that the boards could serve as external frames for smaller circuit boards (Fig. 12-5), eliminating much of the heavy steel frames used heretofore. Note that the horizontal circuit board may be as small or as large as required

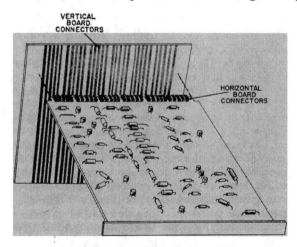

VERTICAL BOARD CONNECTORS

HORIZONTAL BOARD CONNECTORS

Fig. 12-5. Module-assembly construction.

167

for the circuit application. In the illustration it is quite large, containing enough circuitry to possibly make up an entire register. Using the printed-circuit motif, even the connectors are printed and then heavily overlaid with a low-resistance metal (gold, in some cases). The vertical boards serve as frames, with connectors printed in heavy lines. Clamp-like pins join the boards and results in very low-resistance electrical connections.

Although the illustration shows only one horizontal board attached to the vertical "frame" board, many horizontal boards are used in actual practice, forming a series of layers. It is through size-reduction techniques such as this that some computers which formerly required a huge room can now be manufactured in a single, desk-size cabinet.

The printed-circuit board module assembly makes it possible to remove single boards quickly, without the necessity of unsoldering connecting leads, with the accompanying possibility of mixing them up later. The boards slip out of their clamp-pin holders easily, and as soon as they are removed from the frame the printed-circuit connectors are automatically opened. Since the boards can be reinserted in only one way, the correct connections are automatically made when the boards are replaced. The components are readily accessible for testing, repair, and/or replacement.

Another feature of the module assembly is the testing of individual boards in maintenance testers. After the board is removed, it can be placed in the correct slot in the tester, where the connectors of both the board and the tester make contact. This feature will be discussed further in the next chapter.

Assembly Problems. One of the most striking advantages of tight module-assembly packaging in computers is the increased component density. In other words, when circuit boards are packed closely together, more components can be placed within a given space. This tight packing, however, may bring on heat problems, since there is less opportunity for air circulation to cool the circuitry. Adequate cooling can be accomplished by a certain optimum spacing of boards and by using forced-air circulation. This will keep the boards from warping which might cause shorting of components. Vibration or movement of the assembly might also cause shorting. This problem can be solved, at least in part, by coating components with encapsulating compound and clipping the bare "pig-tail" ends very close to the board.

The circuit boards in some computers are alternated with ribbed cooling sheets which are hollow and through which flows a coolant. Some attempts have been made at potting the

168

board modules after assembly since certain epoxies conduct heat more readily than the surrounding air.

Printed circuits are finding increased usage in computers. Although the printed-circuit boards have contributed significantly toward machine efficiency, the computer packaging program has continued with still other techniques—all seeking faster circuits, less volume, lighter weight, reduced power, greater reliability, and increased economy.

Tube-Type Plug-In Circuits

This method of packaging places conventional circuit components between the vacuum tube and its socket (Fig. 12-6). The "chassis" for each individual circuit is made up of a conventional tube socket at the top, a tube base at the bottom, and with solder lugs in between. The entire assembly is held together either by insulated strips or by the components them-

Fig. 12-6. Tube-type plug-in counter circuit.

selves. The latter are soldered to the lugs in a manner to conform to the cylinder-shape of the plug-in circuit. An insulating sleeve (not shown) is slipped over some assemblies. The vacuum tube is plugged into the socket on top and the entire assembly inserted into the chassis tube socket. All that remains to complete the overall circuit connections is simple under-chassis wiring. When a circuit fails, the entire plug-in assembly is removed and a good unit substituted.

Counter Plug-in Circuit. This circuit (Fig. 12-7) is a high-speed flip-flop used for both counting and frequency division. It can accommodate binary counting, AC and DC resetting, counting with feedback, and conventional binary operation at frequencies up to 1 mc or higher. One of these circuits can drive another identical unit without the need for intermediate amplifiers. With a filament supply of 6.3 VAC at 450 ma (external supply), and a plate supply of 200 VDC at 15.2 ma, the circuit can provide an output of 54 volts, peak-to-peak (from +138 to +192, with no load). For frequencies from 0 to 600 kc, it requires a negative 50-volt, 0.4-μsec input pulse or square wave applied to pin 6.

Transistor-Type Plug-in Circuits

Like the tube-type circuit, this package also plugs into a conventional tube socket (Fig. 12-8). The transistor proper may be either plugged into its own tiny socket soldered in place with the other components, or the transistor leads themselves may be soldered directly to the lugs in the assembly. Since the

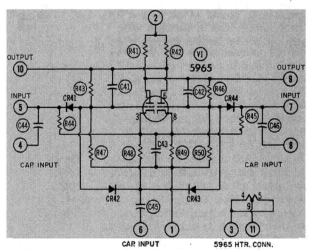

Fig. 12-7. Schematic of a tube-type plug-in counter circuit.

entire unit with transistor in place takes up no more room than an ordinary vacuum tube (as may be seen in the illustration), this type of plug-in circuit has permitted considerable size and weight reduction in computer packaging. The features are the same as those of the tube-type, with the added advantage of considerable power saving as well as the weight and size reduction.

Emitter-Follower Plug-in Circuit. The schematic of the plug-in unit shown in Fig. 12-8 is given in Fig. 12-9. The circuit is a PNP emitter-follower, with a minimum output impedance for negative-going signals. It provides current gain and circuit isolation, and is also used to increase the load-driving capacity ·

170

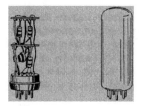

Fig. 12-8. The size of a transistor plug-in circuit compared to a vacuum tube.

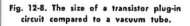

PLUG IN CIRCUIT   VACUUM TUBE

of an input signal. The most popular application for this type of circuit is for operating into DC logic. The emitter-follower shown has a signal frequency-range from DC through 250 kc. (If output signal-amplitude reduction can be tolerated, it may be used up to 500 kc.) The standard input signal generally comes from a conventional flip-flop output whose DC-level may shift from −11 to −3 VDC. In the event it is necessary to provide even greater signal swings, this emitter-follower can accommodate a pulse input of 12 volts peak-to-peak, in which case, the input should be applied through an external capacitor. The output amplitude will be equal to the input signal at all times, but a ¼-volt shift in signal level results, however, in the positive direction for all outputs. *Note that all input and output lines terminate in numbered circles representing socket pin numbers.*

Flat-Board Plug-in Circuit

As a step in conserving space, the printed-circuit board with heavily-plated "tongue" contacts is used, permitting the entire board to be plugged into an appropriate socket (Fig. 12-10).

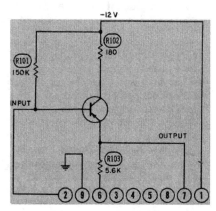

Fig. 12-9. Schematic of a typical transistor plug-in circuit.

171

The shaded areas on the board represent the printed circuit. The leads of conventional components are inserted in the tiny holes which terminate at the printed-circuit lines, and are soldered. (Generally dip-soldering is used, permitting the entire board to be soldered in mere seconds.) The transistors are plugged into tiny sockets which have been soldered onto the board.

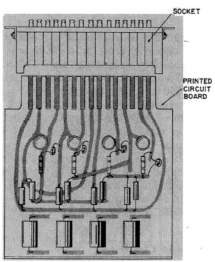

Fig. 12-10. A flat, single-shot multivibrator plug-in circuit board.

The components are the transistor-type plug-in circuits, but the printed wiring occupies less space than conventional circuit wires. Besides, the major dimensional shape of the circuit is flat, rather than cylindrical. Even the connector is flat, with the contacts strung out in a single line. The prongs on the end of the printed-circuit board act as male connector pins. Since the flat connector sockets may be placed so close together that the flat circuit boards almost touch each other, the component density can be greatly increased, making for more efficient packaging.

Single-Shot Flat-Board Plug-in Circuit. The schematic diagram, Fig. 12-11, shows a medium-speed general-purpose single-shot multivibrator. This circuit is useful in timing and computing systems where it may be used for pulse-shaping, fixed-frequency division, generating time delays, pulse-sorting, and

172

for analog counting. The input is a negative trigger whose frequency depends on the pulse-width adjustment and duty cycle. (The maximum duty cycle is approximately 65%.) The outputs may be positive and/or negative pulses. The width of the output pulse is adjustable from 10 μsecs to approximately 30 milliseconds by an external timing capacitor (Cx). Without this external capacitor the pulse width is minimum (approximately 3 μsecs at the 250-kc trigger rate). Note the four NPN

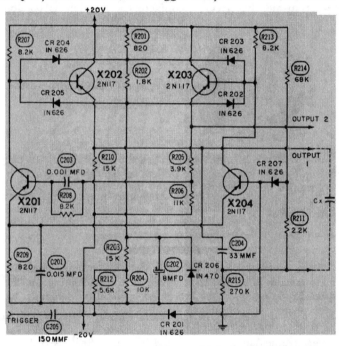

Fig. 12-11. Schematic of the single-shot multivibrator shown in Fig. 12-10.

silicon transistors—two in the single-shot circuit and two acting as emitter-followers. Special features of this circuit include upper- and lower-level clamping of collector voltages, as well as the use of a zener diode to establish reference voltages. (See Schmitt trigger, Chapter 9.)

MECHANIZATION AND AUTOMATION

Because of the large number of circuits (often thousands of nearly identical circuits in a computer), much thought has been given to mechanizing their assembly. Although sporadic attempts at complete automation of the assembly process has been attempted, it is likely that it will be limited to specific operations for some time to come. In the case of thin-film deposited circuitry, however, the outlook for automation is more promising. This field will be discussed later in this chapter.

In the mechanization of packaging, component manufacturers have co-operated and changed their component packaging (Fig. 12-12) to aid the circuit manufacturer as much as possible.

Fig. 12-12. Component packaging for automation.

Notice that the ¼-watt resistors are shown attached to a paper belt much like machine-gun bullets in aircraft. The paper belt is wrapped on a spool. In this way the resistors may be picked up by mechanical fingers and fitted into holes or slots of circuit boards.

PROTECTION

Since computers are frequently used for military operations, some consideration must be given to the packaging for these specialized applications. Increased reliability demands have been placed on computer equipment and certain recommendations have been made for environmental protection, since the equipment might be used in actual warfare. It is important that the electronic devices be protected from the effects of moisture, salt spray, oils, and fuels. The equipment must be thermally protected from external heat. (This requires a material with low thermal conductivity to insulate and protect those sensitive parts which could suffer from thermal degradation.) The equipment must also be insulated from the internal heat generated by the components themselves. For this purpose an encapsulant with high thermal conductivity is recommended. Similarly, it is necessary to protect parts from the mechanical stress of severe shock by damping the mechanical vibrations. Destructive corona discharge can be reduced by the elimination of air surrounding the offending part. To provide this

174

protection a program embracing the rapidly expanding plastic arts soon found acceptability in computer circles. Out of this program came the component "potting" or embedment method, which was a very practical solution to these problems.

Plastic Embedment

One of the first electrical components to be potted was tape-wound cores used in magnetic-core logic (Fig. 12-13). A high-permeability metal tape (mu-metal or similar) is wound around a ceramic material forming an efficient closed-loop metal core. Several windings are thus wound on this core, making up a

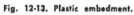

Fig. 12-13. Plastic embedment.

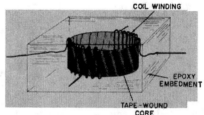

toroid transformer. Two windings with their ends emerging are shown in the illustration. The entire transformer is suspended in a box-like form into which an embedment-plastic is poured. When the epoxy resin sets, the form is removed and the wire ends are ready to be soldered into the appropriate circuits. Virtually any component or even entire, preconnected circuits can be embedded in this manner. A list of terms used in conjunction with potting is shown below.

EMBEDMENT: Entirely enclosing the components of a package with a potting resin that is free-flowing during assembly. The resin fills all the air-voids around the components. It also fills and assumes the shape of the mold (which may be used repeatedly).

ENCAPSULATION: The process of packaging in which the potting compound is applied to the component by dipping, spreading, or spraying. Except for the thickness of the potting material, the component retains its approximate original shape.

IMPREGNATION: The process of thoroughly soaking of the component itself, as well as filling the voids. The encapsulating fluids used are low-viscosity compounds, with the process sometimes being performed in a vacuum to assure complete penetration.

175

POTTING: A plastic process similar to embedment, except the mold becomes an integral part of the outside package of the component. Thus the mold is not re-usable. The mold itself is generally pre-shaped for identification of the final component, allowing automatic identification immediately after potting.

Plastic Processing

Different plastic materials used for packaging require different hardening techniques. The hardening or setting process is called *curing*. When the plastic material is mixed with a hardener, the resulting chemical action frequently generates internal heat. This chemical effect is called an *exothermic reaction*. If the volume of certain types of plastic is great enough, sufficient exothermic heat is generated to damage some particular electronic components. Thus, the design of the package must include consideration of this exotherm that will occur during processing, as well as the convenience of the unit after completion. Other compounds cure slowly at room temperature and with such a low exothermic reaction that it can hardly be noted. Of course, this means the assemblies must be left undisturbed, taking up space, while curing takes place. This could be a mixed blessing. Some plastics have neither of these disadvantages, but do show toxic actions in free air, requiring venting hoods or venting ovens during processing. Generally speaking though, techniques of plastic packaging have happily

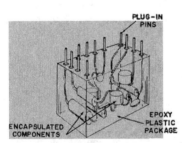

Fig. 12-14. Epoxy-embedded core-driver plug-in unit.

wedded chemistry and electronics to provide improved computer assemblies. With the advent of the "throw-away" philosophy of certain military agencies whose strategic operations do not permit either stocking components or space for repair, a successful attempt was made to package electronic circuitry in a small, plastic-encased unit which would plug in like a vacuum tube (Fig. 12-14). This circuit would either work or

176

it wouldn't (GO or NO-GO), and if it wouldn't, could be thrown away and replaced with a good unit. The electrical components were supported in a temporary jig, soldered, had plug-in pins connected, then the entire unit (surrounded by a mold) was dipped into an encapsulating compound. When the epoxy resin was hard, the entire plastic-coated unit was lifted from the mold, providing a semi-transparent circuit package which could be plugged in like a vacuum tube. Quite a bit of circuitry was enclosed in the embedded circuit. The illustration shows a complete core driver contained in a block whose largest dimension is not over two inches.

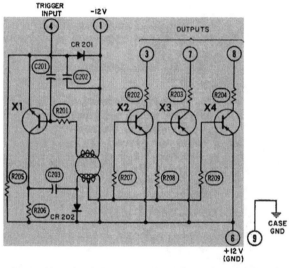

Fig. 12-15. Schematic of the epoxy-embedded core-driver plug-in circuit.

Core Driver Embedded Circuit. This core driver (Fig. 12-15) provides three separate shift-pulse outputs, any one of which can generate standard current-pulses which may be used for shifting data in shift registers (serially connected). A series-tuned circuit incorporating a transistor switch with regeneration makes up the basic circuit of this shift-pulse driver. The tuned circuit (built around T1) provides an output pulse which initially swings negative. By flywheel action that negative swing tends to start oscillation at the resonant frequency of the tuned circuit. At a specific reference level, however, the positive swing is clipped. The net effect produces a pulse at

177

the base of the driving transistors, X2, X3, and X4, resulting in standard current pulses through them.

The core driver requires an input voltage pulse of 10 ±4 volts at a frequency range of 0 to 250 kc. The input pulse must have a minimum width of 1 μsec. If the circuit is resistively loaded to obtain a 100-ma pulse, the output (measured at ½ amplitude) will be 1 ±0.2 μsec wide with a rise time of 0.2 μsec and a fall time of 0.3 μsec.

Repairable Epoxy Embedment

After some experience with embedded components and circuitry, both as units to be soldered into circuits and as com-

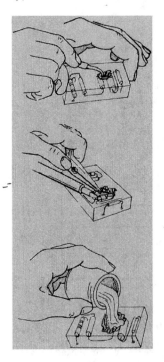

(A) Cutting into the unit.

(B) Removal of faulty component.

(C) Replasticizing the repaired unit.

Fig. 12-16. Repairable epoxy-embedded unit.

plete circuits to be plugged into frames, the problem of what action to take with faulty assemblies once again arose. The "throw away" philosophy was fine as long as simple, inexpensive units were involved. When entire circuits costing up to

178

$100 and more were imbedded, management raised an eyebrow when told the unit would be thrown away if a single component in it became faulty. Accordingly, packaging techniques using epoxy resins for embedment, yet permitting limited repairs, were evolved (Fig. 12-16).

The repairable unit contains pre-wired components, as in any similar embedment, but in order to permit repairs it must also:

1. Provide access points (such as pins) to permit isolation of faults to single components.
2. Be pre-assembled in such a manner that removal of a single component is possible without destroying the entire module.
3. Use a plastic compound of such a nature that it can be cut into (or dissolved) and removed without damaging the module.
4. Permit plastic refilling after the component repair has been completed.

One of the most practical techniques of reaching a faulty component in a repairable epoxy embedment is to cut into the plastic with a scalpel, as shown in Fig. 12-16A. Careful cutting or chipping will remove the plastic material from the desired area. (There are other methods of plastic removal, such as by chemical "strippers" having an action similar to paint-remover, but this type of repair is generally performed at large depots or at the factory.)

After the faulty component is made accessible, it is removed and a good part is soldered in place in the usual way (Fig. 12-16B). The components are then gently positioned to avoid shorting, after which the module is tested either in the circuit involved or in a maintenance tester. If the repair is satisfactory, a small batch of epoxy resin is mixed with a suitable hardener, and poured into the opened module (Fig. 12-16C). When the plastic cures, the bond is complete.

Because of the involved cutting and later plasticizing, even the repairable epoxy embedment suffers from relatively high maintenance cost. However, it is a necessary adjunct of the mechanical, electrical, and thermal isolation required by certain military and commercial equipment applications.

THIN FILMS

Probably the greatest promise of fulfillment of practical packaging of computer circuits into a really small space has been

179

made with the development of thin films. This process, less than 10 years old at this writing, has been variously called *miniaturization* and *micro-miniaturization*. What the transistor did to permit reduction in size from vacuum-tube construction, the thin-film technique did to permit entire circuits to fit into the same space occupied by a single transistor. The entire concept of size has to be readjusted when thinking of thin films.

Think of a typical flip-flop circuit using a twin-triode tube (already a space reduction over two separate triodes) with associated resistors, capacitors, wiring, and chassis, and picture the smallest size in which it could be accommodated. Now look at Fig. 12-17 and see the practical size of a flip-flop fabricated with thin films. This is the real thing. It works!

Fig. 12-17. Relative size of a thin-film flip-flop circuit.

Just what is the thin-film story? Can a scrap of cigarette-wrapper foil be shaped into a practical electronic circuit? Would it require special equipment? How would such a circuit be serviced when the soldering-iron tip touches more than one component, no matter how small you make the tip? This is an entirely new type of circuit thinking, and quite an adjustment has to be made to understand it.

Thin-Film Maintenance

To begin with, the soldering iron is no longer practical for thin-film repair. Not only is the iron tip too large to handle the micro-miniature thin-film circuitry, but even if the iron were small enough, the heat generated would undoubtably destroy the circuit before the connection could be soldered. Maintenance of thin films then, takes on a whole new aspect. Repair in the field is impossible, so replacement is the only procedure. Even signal-tracing by conventional techniques is impossible. How can a voltage reading be obtained if the test probe covers more than one terminal? Besides, the pressure of the probe would probably crush the thin-film circuit, ruining it. Thus, design problems have to be worked out giving consideration to the smallest practical module size for replacement.

Since it is agreed that the individual component cannot be checked in the field, wholly new concepts in maintenance have had to be formulated. These are covered in the next chapter. Suffice it to say for now, however, that only circuits can be checked, *not individual components*. As a matter of fact, certain individual components cannot even be *seen* since inter-component relationships provide capacity and inductance, and in some instances the connections between components even provide the resistance required.

Appearance of Thin Films

An enlarged cross-section of a thin-film unit is shown in Fig. 12-18. The substrate is the insulating base, possibly glass, upon which a thin film of conducting material is deposited. Even though shown magnified in the illustration, the thin-film thick-

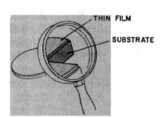

Fig. 12-18. Enlarged cross-section of a substrate showing the thin-film deposit.

ness has been exaggerated for visibility. Some films are so thin they are nearly transparent, being only a few atoms thick. The substrate shown in the illustration is the thinnest glass which can be used without breaking in handling. (Actually, the limiting factor of thin-film devices is the fragility of the substrates. How thin can it be?) Most thin films look like tiny mirrors when viewed through a magnifying glass, since the deposited films are almost always silvery in appearance.

Thin-film Dynamic Devices

Semiconductors can also be deposited in thin-film form (Fig. 12-19). Using the same extremely thin substrate (glass, or similar substance), a single-crystal semiconductor is deposited to form the transistor base. Later, other component elements will be deposited on that thin film to provide the emitter and collector. Also shown in the illustration is a thin-film conducting ring also which might serve as a connecting lead from the emitter (to be deposited later). The substrate shape illustrated is circular. In actual practice, the substrate could take any flat form, generally rectangular.

181

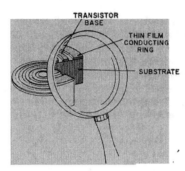

TRANSISTOR
BASE

THIN FILM
CONDUCTING
RING

SUBSTRATE

Fig. 12-19. Enlarged cross-section of a substrate showing the deposited dynamic devices.

To picture thin-film fabrication, imagine painting a pattern through a very tiny stencil (Fig. 12-20). A number of screening masks are first fabricated by photo-etching an extremely thin sheet of stainless steel or similar metal. The entire group of masks shown in the illustration is not much larger than ¼ inch in the maximum dimension! The screening mask is laid over the clean substrate and the two are temporarily taped together. They are then placed under a bell jar in a vacuum chamber, along with a small quantity of the metal to be deposited held over an electric heating coil. A vacuum is then formed in the chamber, and the heating coil is energized, vaporizing the metal. This vapor fills the bell jar, and settles through the openings of the screening mask onto the surface of the substrate. At a controlled time the process is stopped, the vacuum is released, and the screening mask is removed. The substrate now has the required thin-film deposited on it in just the correct shape and thickness.

Succeeding screens are taped on, and other thin-film materials are deposited, usually alternating conducting (metal) films with insulating (oxide) films. Control of the film thickness may be achieved by shining a light through the vaporized material in the vacuum chamber and using this light to operate a photo-

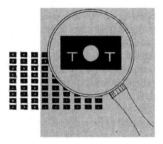

Fig. 12-20. Screening-mask detail.

cell, which in turn, controls the depositing process. Since everything in the vacuum chamber will have a film deposited upon it, the light read by the photocell will gradually diminish as the deposit increases until the pre-determined cut-off point is reached. Other thickness-measurement methods include vibrating devices, the faces of which receive a portion of the film deposition, damping their oscillation. This change in the amplitude of vibration is measured and used to control the deposit thickness.

The explanation of the thin-film deposition has, of course, been greatly simplified. Actually, the operation of devices in a vacuum is complex, requiring chemists for the metal composition, physicists for the operation planning, and electronic-circuit designers for the major design conversions from the use of large, separate components, to the thin-film representations. For those who like quantitative figures, some representative values envolved in thin films might be of interest. The first layer might be a film of copper 3,000 Angstrom (approximately .00001 in) thick to represent the "printed-circuit wiring." The next layer might be a similar thickness of insulating material, such as silicon monoxide (SiO), deposited through a masking screen hiding those parts of the first layer that must join the third layer. The third layer might be any metallic compound a few Angstroms thick, joining the conducting lines of the first layer, but insulated from other parts of the first layer by the second insulating layer. In this way, succeeding layers can be deposited until the entire circuit has been fabricated. Note that the connections between "components" are *deposited* together, instead of soldering. The final thickness of the several layers in simple circuits is usually not much more than 0.001 inch.

Multi-Layer Fabrication. The alternation of conducting and insulating areas of thin films provides a multi-layer module such as that shown in Fig. 12-21. Note that connecting leads have been attached for connection to other circuitry. This can be done by special spot-welding, special soldering techniques, or even by special cold-solder-paste techniques. Note also that the entire circuit is not much larger than a dime, which is shown for comparison. It is difficult to see the several layers involved, but they are all there. In the very center is the dynamic module, which is fabricated separately and then assembled with the entire circuit as the last step of the operation.

The fabrication of the thin-film flip-flop shown is started with a substrate upon which is deposited alternate layers of conducting and insulating materials. The shape of each thin-film layer is determined by the screening mask attached to the sub-

183

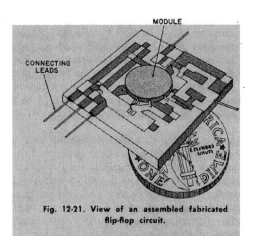

Fig. 12-21. View of an assembled fabricated
flip-flop circuit.

strate before deposition is started. Note in Fig. 12-22 how the
different circuit components are fabricated.

Three controlled layers (Fig. 12-22A) provide a capacitor.
(Only a portion of the substrate is shown.) At the same time
the three layers produce a capacitor, the remainder of the mask
is providing other components. For example, in Fig. 12-22B, a
single layer (it could be the first, third, fifth, or any other) generates the connection between conductors which would continue on to other connections. One way to make inductances is
shown in Fig. 12-22C. At higher frequencies, the proximity of
the components may introduce sufficient inductance to provide

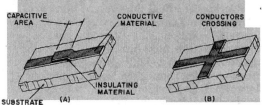

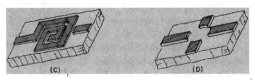

Fig. 12-22. Thin-film component fabrication.

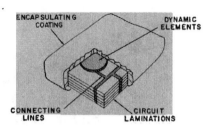

Fig. 12-23. Laminated-circuit
module detail.

ENCAPSULATING
COATING

DYNAMIC
ELEMENTS

CONNECTING
LINES

CIRCUIT
LAMINATIONS

a "phantom" coil. Where static components, such as conducting lines, capacitors, and coils join other dynamic components to be added later, a termination such as that shown in Fig. 12-22D may be used.

Under certain conditions the thin-film circuit "sheet" can be laid against similar sheets, with connecting lines soldered between them so that the laminated series forms a module (Fig. 12-23). The dynamic elements, fabricated separately, are added to these sheets, and the entire unit may then be encapsulated to make a complete module. This module may be terminated in plug-in pins, or be soldered in place with extended connecting leads. In the example shown, a series of circuits are encapsulated in one package, perhaps taking up the space normally occupied by a single conventional component in ordinary circuitry. An alternate plastic potting technique is shown in Fig. 12-24. Here each "sheet" is made in disc form, with connection leads brought out separately. Those discs to be connected together are first factory-soldered. Then the entire series of *sandwiches* are dipped into a potting compound. This new potted unit can be considered as a single component for use in conventional circuitry. Some high-quality capacitors made in this fashion for tight-space utilization in conventional circuits are already on the market. To provide maximum space utilization, the dynamic elements are made as separate modules. The module shown in Fig. 12-25 must perform the same function as two separate transistors and two diodes. Of course, the "insides" of two transistors and two diodes could be interconnected and potted as a unit. This, however, is not thin films.

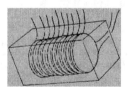

Fig. 12-24. Potted laminated
thin-film circuits.

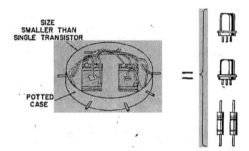

Fig. 12-25. A fabricated transistor dual-diode
module and its equivalent.

Even greater miniaturization is possible using thin-film techniques. The circuit making up the central module in a flip-flop
is shown in Fig. 12-26. Note that a diode is connected to each
base. In fabrication, two separate substrates each get identical
deposition for the first layer emitter, then a semiconductor
single-crystal base layer. This completes the thin-film portion.
Leads are now connected, and collector and diode points sol-

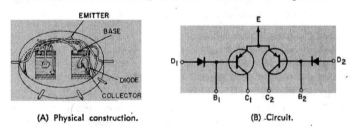

(A) Physical construction.   (B) Circuit.

Fig. 12-26. A fabricated transistor dual-diode module.

dered to the crystalline thin film. From this point on tiny conventional leads are added and brought out for later connections.
The potting completes the module, which now contains all the
dynamic portions of the flip-flop circuit to come.

In a separate operation, a thin glass substrate with a hole in
the center is prepared for a 4-layer, thin-film deposition (Fig.
12-27). The hole in the substrate is for the module already prepared in the separate operation. The first layer is the conducting metal, providing intra-circuit wiring and capacitor plates.
The next layer is also a conducting metal, but of greater resis-
tivity (thinner deposition). The next layer of SiO provides insulation in general and dielectric for the capacitors in particular. The final layer of conducting metal makes up the sec-

186

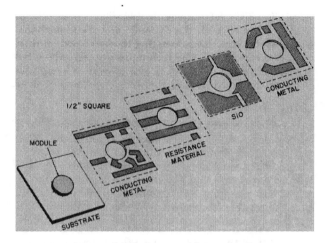

Fig. 12-27. Exploded view of a fabricated flip-flop.

ond plate of the capacitors and the final wiring and terminating points. Although it appears there are five sheets in the illustration, there is really only one with four thin-film layers deposited upon it. The completed static substrate is now connected with the center dynamic module making up a complete flip-flop, the schematic of which is shown in Fig. 12-28.

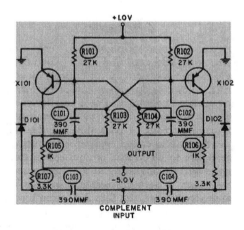

Fig. 12-28. Schematic of a fabricated
flip-flop circuit.

187

More advanced techniques in thin-film fabrication make it possible to deposit both the dynamic and static portions of the circuitry at the same time, avoiding the awkward, multiple-step process described here. The technique just described, however, is a good, practical one, and it also permits a simple analysis because of the separation of the different steps involved.

Thin-Film Problems

It is a paradox that thin-film modules fabricated for plug-in operation are limited by the plug-in connections. The entire circuit module is generally smaller than the pins which connect it to the other sections! Besides, the complex operations involved in packaging and soldering the leads and the strength required for plugging and un-plugging make it advisable to reduce the number of connecting points to a minimum. Accordingly, thin-film fabrication strives to embrace as much of the circuitry as it can in a single substrate sheet. This increases the practicability of the operation since the vacuum-chamber operation is a costly and time-consuming process. Complicated automatic controls are all constructed inside the vacuum chamber so that once the original substrate is inserted, and the machine is pumped down to the required vacuum, the repeated deposition cycles are run without interruption. This makes for greater reliability, less contamination, and reduced cost. At this writing, however, thin-film fabrication is probably the most expensive circuit technique in use.

CRYOGENICS

It has been found that at extremely low temperatures, resistance decreases to nearly zero and can be modified by applied magnetic fields. This has opened an entirely new field of circuitry in which computer operation can be performed with the smallest components imaginable. These smaller components are made possible by the low-temperature environment which permits the required current to pass through the thinnest films that can be made. This is called *cryogenic* operation and is particularly applicable to electronic equipment in missiles where the components will be operating at a temperature of absolute zero in outer space. Where cryogenic operation is desired in conventional environments, the thin-film circuitry is suspended in huge *Thermos*-like bottles in which liquid helium or other gases maintain the required temperature. Entirely different switching methods are possible under cryogenic environments, although conventional circuits are also used where practicable.

188

REVIEW QUESTIONS

1. Why are transistorized computer circuits packaged on smaller printed-circuit boards?

2. Why is modular construction always used in computers?

3. What types of plug-in circuits are used?

4. What production techniques are used to protect plug-in circuits from moisture, shorting, shock, and other physical damage?

5. How are thin-film modules fabricated?

CHAPTER 13

Computer Module Maintenance

The modular packaging of computers has brought many changes in maintenance techniques. Since the dread of "down time" lies so heavily upon the maintenance personnel, they usually keep a stock of replacement modules. The moment a fault develops and is localized, the offending module is removed and a replacement inserted, always striving, above all, to restore service immediately. Between operational maintenance times, the maintenance personnel have an opportunity to test and repair the faulty modules. Ideally, a module should be tested in a known, operating equipment. Thus, if the equipment operates normally when the module is inserted in place, then that module is good. If the resulting equipment operation is not normal, however, then that module must be faulty. Since the computer is not generally available to maintenance personnel for checking suspected modules, a tester is provided.

MODULE-BOARD TESTER

Where standard module-boards are to be tested, a board socket is provided on a test bench (Fig. 13-1). The plug-in board is placed in the socket, as shown. Switching arrangements are provided to allow testing different size and type boards. In this manner the board is connected with circuitry in the test bench, with suitable voltages and signals available to activate the plugged-in circuits. The instrument meter indicates the values of selected currents, while the digital voltmeter provides precise indications of selected outputs. A file of GO/NO-GO requirements permit the maintenance personnel to determine if the selected board meets instrument specifications. In the event the tested board proves faulty, additional switching arrangements are provided to permit checking voltages and currents

191

from input to output at selected points, which rapidly localizes the trouble to individual component(s) without the necessity of hay-wire connections to various test instruments. These module testers ride on large rubber-covered casters in large installations, providing prompt, silent maintenance checking. Similar testers check entire module-frame drawers. Some have extension leads to go directly into the computer in order to reach hard-to-get terminals. These testers provide entire circuit dynamic-tests simulating actual operation of the computer.

TRANSISTOR CURVE-TRACER

Rivalling the module testers, ornate console-type equipment provide a battery of tests upon individual transistors, producing a visual readout on an oscilloscope screen. See Fig. 13-2. The transistor to be tested is placed in a socket (on the horizontal

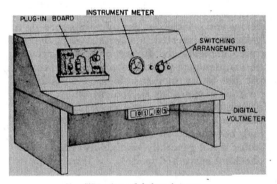

Fig. 13-1. A module-board tester.

bench-portion of the console). External switches select appropriate potentials while built-in switching equipment and oscillators apply the necessary signals to test the transistor paramenters. Multiple-scanning sweep-switches cause a family of response curves to appear on the screen. Where production checking is performed on similar units, the proper trace can be drawn upon a plastic overlay which is then placed on the screen, permitting an instant GO/NO-GO check of the transistor under test.

A simplified schematic diagram of a transistor curve-tracer is shown in Fig. 13-3. The H output provides oscilloscope horizontal sweep directly proportional to variations in the transistor collector *voltage*. (To avoid interference from the scope's

192

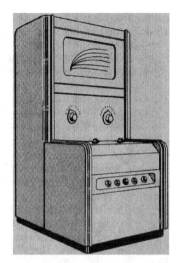

Fig. 13-2. A transistor curve-tracer.

internal horizontal sweep circuits, turn them off). The V output provides a vertical deflection which is directly proportional to the variations in collector *current*. Since change of current is applied to one set of deflection plates and change of voltage to the other set, the resultant display on the scope is the collector voltage-current characteristic curve. The detailed operation is as follows:

The common-emitter mode is used, as shown in the diagram. Note that this is the *test* transistor providing its own output. The desired family of curves required is for varying base-currents. If switch S1 is placed in the open position, as shown,

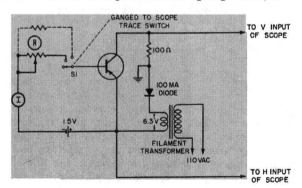

Fig. 13-3. Simplified schematic of a transistor curve-tracer.

base current will be zero. At this time, the vertical- and horizontal-gain controls of the scope are adjusted to obtain the desired image size and starting at the lower portion of the screen. (This is the lowest of the family of characteristic curves.) Now, if S1 is switched to another position, the resistor R can be adjusted for the next curve desired. Repeating this procedure, separate curves will be displayed. To obtain the *entire* family of curves at one time, the different settings of the base resistor are replaced by fixed resistances, each being switched into the circuit at the proper time by the same circuit which switches the trace on the scope. For the first instant that the scope is making a sweep, the curve-trace circuitry switches an open circuit for the base. This provides the lowest trace. The next instant the scope switch starts to make another trace, simultaneously switching in a suitable resistance in the base circuit to provide the lowest base-current curve desired. The screen phosphor holds the first curve image while this new trace appears on the screen. Repetitive sweeps switch different base resistances, making the whole family of curves appear on the screen. The detailed mechanics of switching the different base resistances are omitted here. A transparent scale showing known voltages previously applied to the horizontal and vertical inputs can be laid over the screen to translate the scope curves to real abscissas and ordinates. Alternatively, the image of the curves can be modified to fit the standard reticule available for most scopes. Here, the absolute values can be read from the previously calibrated reticule graduations. To check an NPN transistor, the connections to the battery and to the 6-volt rectifier diode are reversed.

TRANSISTOR PARAMETER TESTS

Saturation Gain Test

A large series resistance R (Fig. 13-4) makes the power supply act as a constant-current source, adjusted by R to the specified emitter current required. The collector-base voltage, V_{CB}, may be read by voltmeter V, and adjusted to manufacturer's specs by the 10K potentiometer. By definition, transistor saturation is expressed when V_{CB} is reduced to zero, at which time the current gain tested represents saturation current gain, h_{FE}. The values of resistance in the test are so selected that saturation current gain can be read directly from the 10K potentiometer dial when the appropriate 10K fixed resistor is switched into the circuit. Both PNP and NPN transistors can be tested by merely reversing power supply polarity.

194

Junction Leakage and Breakdown Test

Reversing the polarity of the power supply provides a check for both PNP and NPN transistors. A variable-voltage power supply (Fig. 13-5) is used to apply a reverse bias to the collector-base junction of the test transistor through a 50K resistor

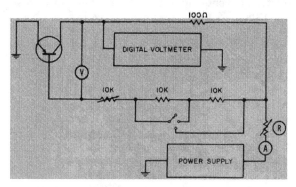

Fig. 13-4. Transistor saturation-current gain test (h_FE).

(used as a current limiter in case of transistor failure). Where excess currents cause too much voltage drop across that resistor, a switch is used to by-pass it. As the power-supply voltage is varied, collector-base junction breakdown-voltage BV (CBO) is indicated on the digital voltmeter. That reading is the reverse-bias required to provide the specified leakage (break-

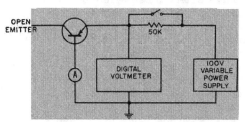

Fig. 13-5. Transistor-junction leakage and breakdown test.

down) current (which can be read at A) when the emitter is left open. For the measurement of emitter-base junction breakdown, the emitter and collector leads are reversed. As in the saturation-gain test, both PNP and NPN transistors can be checked by providing the proper polarity from the power supply.

Minority-Carrier Storage Test

Switching speed of transistors is limited by, among other factors, storage time (V_{st}). The minority-carrier storage is measured, not by clock time, but by the analog of its V_{st} (Fig. 13-6). The diagram shows a PNP under test. Assuming no input, the transistor is conducting because of the $-XV$ base supply through the 20K resistor. This provides forward bias which, if great enough, will cause the transistor to saturate. Its effective collector-emitter impedance is extremely low with the result that the collector voltage is practically zero (voltage measured at the collector, not at the collector supply). The input capacitor

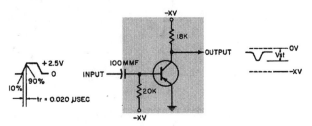

Fig. 13-6. Minority-carrier storage test.

and resistor form a differentiating network causing the input waveform to provide a positive spike which back-biases the base-emitter junction. The length of time it takes the transistor to reach cut off after its initial saturation is the time required for minority carriers to be "swept out" of the base region. In a perfect transistor the storage time would be negligible, causing the output to reach $-XV$ instantly. Since practical storage time does exist, however, the turn-off action is delayed. The negative peak-output voltage, V_{st}, decreases with increased storage time for the fixed duration of the positive input-pulse. Thus, the measure of V_{st} provides a minority-carrier storage-time test. This is an advantage in production testing, since a single voltage reading provides the required time measurement. The preceding tests have shown a few examples of checking transistor quality. Many more are possible, some showing specific quality performance.

Similarly, diodes can be field tested in a number of ways. An ohmmeter placed across the diode, with a reversal of the leads, provides a quick field check. A ratio of at least 100:1 in the back to forward resistance indicates a good unit. A few instrument tests used in production are given below.

196

Reverse Leakage-Current Test

The single diode under test is shown in Fig. 13-7. It is reverse-biased by a variable power supply which is adjusted until the reverse-bias voltage as read on the digital voltmeter is the value specified by the manufacturer. The desired measurement, I_r, can now be read at A. Note that the digital voltmeter is measuring the voltage drop across the ammeter (I) *and* the tested diode at the same time. In this way, the current at A

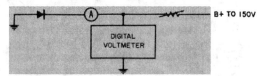

Fig. 13-7. Diode reverse leakage-curernt test (I_r).

does *not* include the current flow through the digital voltmeter, which might distort the final reading.

Forward Voltage-Drop Test

Fig. 13-8 shows a single diode under test. Forward-bias is produced through the potentiometer by the variable power supply, causing the diode to conduct as it normally would in the conventional computer circuit. When the specified current,

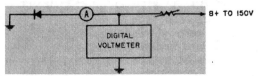

Fig. 13-8. Diode forward voltage-drop test (V_f).

indicated at A, is produced by variation of the potentiometer, the digital voltmeter records the forward voltage-drop, V_f, across the diode.

These forward- and reverse-bias tests for diodes generally supply adequate information. Similar tests can be made for capacitor leakage as well as other qualities of components.

B-H LOOP TESTER

Magnetic cores are frequently used in computers, both for core logic and for memories. The conductivity of the core winding and the inductance of the coil can be checked by normal testing techniques. The permeability of the core, however, is more difficult to test. Permeability (μ) is the ratio of magnetization (B) to magnetic induction (H). This is tested with equipment, shown in Fig. 13-9, which provides the familiar hysteresis curve. The power supply operates the pulse shaper, which in turn, supplies the negative driving-pulses. The R-C network associated with the test core causes the waveform

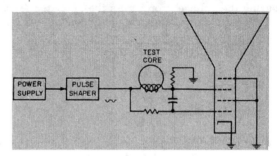

Fig. 13-9. B-H loop tester.

to be integrated. The rise and fall of this integrated waveform is determined by the permeability of the test core, showing up on the associated scope as a B-H curve.

THE PROBLEM OF MAINTENANCE

As the complexity of electronic computers increase it is reasonable to expect that the problem of maintenance will also increase. Put another way, a 500-circuit machine may be five times as difficult to maintain as one containing 100 circuits. Unfortunately, the permissible "down time" of the latest, most complex computers is growing less.

Reliability

The users of the more complex computers are demanding even greater reliability, even though with so much complexity there is much more that can go wrong. For practical figures, one authority states that for 24-hour *continuous* operation the maximum allowable down time is from 0 to 1.0 hour per day. How would *you* like to have to guarantee that a computer containing from 1,000 to 100,000 circuits would operate perfectly for at least 23 out of 24 hours of continuous operation?

This requirement is quite reasonable. Remember that key civilian and military missions are trusted to this most complex of electronic systems. This means that the automatic beacon guiding an aircraft to a blind landing, the radar net identifying and locating hostile aircraft and missiles, the weapons of war and of national defense—all these must operate with maximum reliability. The possibility of failure during an enemy invasion is beyond allowable tolerance. Even equipment cost, long a factor in packaging and design, is overlooked in certain reliability requirements. The most current concept in computer operation assuring maximum reliability involves the following: Confidence indicators to verify tolerable circuit operation to reassure the operator. Automatic fault-finding circuitry, showing lighted indicators to signify circuit faults even before the operator can detect faulty results. Automatic fault-correction circuitry to correct certain limited types of faulty function. Marginal checking and maintenance programs built into the computer to check large operational-block operation quickly during periods of relative lull activity.

Down Time

Much has been said under reliability and the problems of maintenance about *down time*. Just what is it? Down time is generally construed as being the time during which the equipment is not operating at its profitable best. Two basically different kinds of down time are involved—*scheduled* and *unscheduled*. Scheduled down-time does not represent system failure. Equipment operating up to 24 hours per day most certainly must have definite scheduled times for routine servicing, preventive maintenance, and checkout functions. These times are usually set up in advance and scheduled for periods when the equipment is not currently required. Such scheduled down-time is generally considered normal operation.

Unscheduled down time, on the other hand, represents the period between the time of equipment failure and the subsequent restoration to service. A great deal of mathematics has been perpetrated, attempting to show in advance how much unscheduled down-time may be anticipated for various conditions of operation. The important point is—keep the unscheduled down-time *down*.

Diagnostic Programming

A special diagnostic program is either built in as an integral part of the computer or externally applied. This process enables operating personnel, without special skills in maintenance, to have the computer diagnose its own troubles. This is usually performed during scheduled down-time. The program

199

exercises various functions in the computer, checking these for proper operation. If the result of the program is other than expected, the computer automatically institutes an error-locating program. This exercises additional investigating functions, with the computer rendering decisions about the probable location of the error. These additional exercises are called marginal checking programs.

Marginal Checking Program. A circuit is expected to operate between certain upper and lower limits of tolerance. The tolerance of each component is weighed during circuit design to establish the circuit tolerance. Ideally, the circuit operates in the middle of its design-tolerance range. In this way, variations either up or down may be tolerated without circuit failure. The marginal checking program examines circuit operation over the entire tolerance range by running the supply voltages up and down, and by changing the amplitude and frequency of the signal inputs to, and slightly beyond, the full design limits. If the circuit cannot "take it," a failure will result. In this way, forthcoming failures can be predicted during scheduled down-time—a marked advantage in reliability.

Preventive Maintenance

When the program operator sees the confidence indicators failing as the result of the maintenance program, the files which relate confidence indicators to specific circuit modules are checked. If maintenance personnel are not present, the operator can replace the suspected module with an available stock replacement. Immediately afterward the operator re-runs the diagnostic program. If it now shows normal results, the fault is presumed corrected. At the end of the scheduled down-time, the computer is restored to normal service without unscheduled down-time being charged.

Marginal-Checking Technique

The entire diagnostic and marginal checking program activity must be completed in a few minutes if high reliability of performance is to be expected. Accordingly, routine checking of circuits, one at a time, is too slow. For speedier checking, circuits are paralleled as shown in Fig. 13-10. Here, a single gate with the four possibilities of inputs is shown. After all four tests have been performed, it can be said that this particular gate is properly checked. If the outputs were logical *1* or *0* as required, then the confidence indicators would remain lighted. Now look at Fig. 13-11. Here, in the same time that the single gate was checked four ways, four different gates can be checked by the same number of circuit combinations. After each check the connections are switched, moving one gate to the next check. This, then, is the marginal-checking technique—switching the various circuits in and out, checking signal and power-supply range, and circuit outputs. Of course,

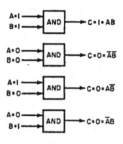

Fig. 13-10. Marginal checking
of AND gates.

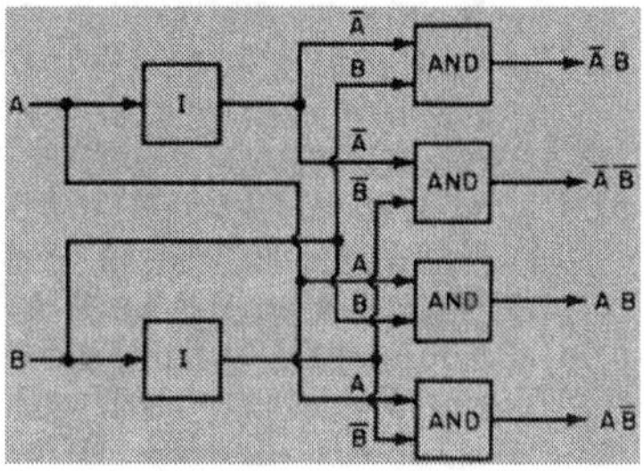

Fig. 13-11. Marginal checking of four
AND gates simultaneously.

this requires additional switching hardware and wiring, but the rapid circuit checking and improved reliability generally warrants it.

Printed Circuits

Certain precautions should be followed in making repairs on printed circuitry. The cramped space, small components, and fragile connecting leads require special treatment. Listed below are general procedures that should be followed.

1. Use insulated probes to move components. Metallic probes may perforate insulation or damage the printed circuitry.
2. If metallic probes are used, care must be exercised to avoid shorting components while probing with current on. The close packing of components make it easy to burn out several parts with one careless movement of a metal probe.
3. Small components on printed circuits generally look very much alike. It is difficult to tell a diode from a capacitor or from a resistor. Use ample light and a magnifying glass, if necessary, to identify components. Refer to diagrams to be certain.
4. Caution in soldering is especially urged. Components are so tiny and their insulation so thin that heat from a conventional iron may damage them. Use the smallest prac-

201

tical soldering-iron tip possible. Use a heat sink, if only long-nose pliers, when soldering semiconductor and tantalum capacitor leads.

5. General rules for soldering these circuits are not practical. Do not hold the iron on the joint until it is hot enough to melt the solder unless an adequate heat sink is applied between the joint and the component. Use as little heat as necessary to obtain a satisfactory solder joint and use the absolute minimum of solder, removing any excess. A solder blob is a conductor which can touch a nearby joint and possibly cause damage.

6. When using an ohmmeter for checking continuity, use the highest resistance scale possible to limit battery current. Certain circuit components may be damaged with the battery current used with low-resistance ranges. Check the circuit diagram before indiscriminately probing or checking resistances to see if such measurement might damage the components.

7. Avoid overtightening screws and nuts. Components may crack under the increased pressure. Finger-tightness may be adequate where plastic threads are used.

8. Carefully note the position of a component and its leads before removing from the circuit. Make a sketch, if possible, and tie a tag onto each lead to identify it. Take special care not to dislodge adjacent components while removing the old part.

9. Replace the new component in the same position as the old one, following the sketch and the tags on the leads.

10. Carefully make first a mechanical and then a soldered connection, observing the precautions listed above. Make certain the soldered joint does not touch any other points. Make certain that physical placement of the new part does not interfere with adjacent circuitry.

General Maintenance Techniques. The same general rules for conventional maintenance hold for printed circuits as well. Inspect components and insulation for signs of burning caused by overheating. Check capacitors for leaking wax and connections for faulty contacts. Look for bare metal parts touching others. Inspect connecting lines and cables for continuity. Listen for signs of improper operation, especially when components are moved while current is on. Listen for distortion of audible signals. Check for an odor caused by charred insulation, overheated selenium rectifiers, melted wax, carbonized materials, ozone, etc. While probing, feel if components are firm to

202

the touch, rigidly connected. Use just enough pressure for detection, since too much may do even more damage.

Printed-Circuit Repair Procedure

Because some maintenance men are accustomed to repair of circuits on conventional chassis, similar techniques may be tried on printed circuits. Some modification of these techniques, however, is necessary (Fig. 13-12). Note at (A) how the leads of the suspected component have been cut to remove it. The next step (B) shows how the individual soldered ends are then heated and pulled out from the bottom (or top) without inter-

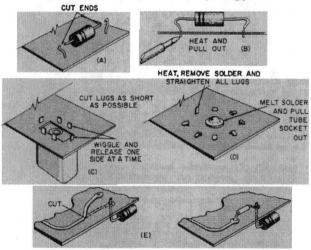

Fig. 13-12. Printed-circuit repair procedures.

ference with the body of the component (already removed). This now permits replacement with a good unit. Where the component is a can (C), the lugs are cut as short as possible before an attempt is made to free the unit. The can is then wiggled as the lugs are heated and one side at a time is released until finally the unit can be removed. Clean the lug slots before replacing with a new can. When removing a tube socket of which all lugs are soldered, heat them one at a time, remove the solder and straighten each lug. Then, heat the center lug and pull the socket out, as shown at (D). Repair of printed-circuit wiring is shown at (E), where the damaged portion is cut, removed, and replaced with a length of conventional wire. Besides the small components mounted pig-tail fashion on the boards, certain switches and potentiometers are also used.

These are sometimes faulty, requiring slight bending of the contact arms. A switch-contact tension tool is shown in Fig. 13-13A. Note that it is offset, making it convenient to reach around parts to manipulate the switch contacts. In use, the slot at the end of the tool is inserted over the thin spring metal to be bent. The tool is turned slightly, giving the spring a slight bend. The other end of the tool can be used as a probe. Fig. 13-13B shows an emergency tension tool made from a sardine-can key. If the tiny potentiometers are noisy a drop of carbon-tetrachloride or similar solvent will often effect a cure.

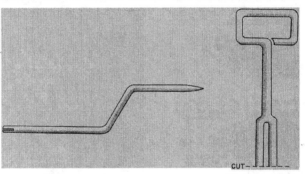

(A) Commercial.   (B) Home made.

Fig. 13-13. Switch-contact tension tools.

Transistor Precautions

A great deal has been said about using care in soldering semiconductors, especially to provide a heat sink or to avoid damage. Other precautions have been listed to which should be added the one concerning the insertion and removal of transistors from their sockets. *Insert and remove transistors from their sockets only when the current is off.* To do otherwise may damage it. Also remember that removing the load from a transistor circuit may affect the current drawn through the transistor, with the possibility of an overload causing damage.

REVIEW QUESTIONS

1. What are module testers?
2. How are module testers used?
3. How do transistor curve-tracers work?
4. How is marginal testing used to improve computer circuit reliability?
5. What is diagnostic programming?

ANSWERS

TO REVIEW QUESTIONS

Chapter 1

1. A computer is a device which processes input data to provide output data representing mathematical relationships between the input data.

2. A computer control system is a device which processes input data concerning the environment in order to provide output data which will cause a desired modification of that environment.

3. (a) Data conversion to electrical quantities. (b) Addition. (c) Subtraction. (d) Multiplication. (e) Division. (f) Comparison. (g) Data transfer. (h) Data storage. (i) Operation sequencing and timing. (j) Yes-no decision-making. (k) Data conversion to desired form.

4. The bi-metallic element of a thermostat; a small voltage generator (tachometer) driven by a rotating shaft; a shaft-driven resistor (potentiometer); a temperature-sensitive voltage generator (thermocouple); a light-sensitive voltage generator (photocell); and a pressure-sensitive voltage generator (piezo-electric crystal or a microswitch).

5. In analog computers numbers are represented by voltages having values equal to the number. In some cases the value of the voltage may be some known fraction of the number.

6. In digital computers, pulses are used to represent numbers. One way is to have one pulse for each unit of the number. Other methods use coded pulses to represent a number.

7. By applying the y input to an amplifier having a gain of 20.

8. $6 + 6 + 6 + 6 = 24$.

9. The distributor provides sequenced voltage pulses to the spark plug of each cylinder. Consider the result when each cylinder is not fired at precisely the right time.

10. Wear Raincoat   Wear Topcoat   Wear Sunglasses and no jacket

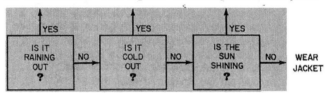

11. The light bulb converts the applied electrical power into illumination or into a visual signal of some condition.

Chapter 2

1. Exact voltages must be used in analog computers to accurately represent numerical quantities. Power supply variations can cause false pulses to be generated in digital computers.

2. Emitter followers provide high input impedances. This prevents excessive load currents from being drawn by successive stages. That is, emitter followers are often used between stages or in the first stages of amplifiers designed to draw very small input currents.

3. Direct-coupled amplifiers are used because they are able to process signals which remain fairly constant over long periods of time. These signals cannot be processed by stages having reactive coupling elements.

4. The 2-diode type and the bridge type.

5. (1) the rectifier, (2) the control circuit, and (3) the regulator.

6. A series regulator acts as a variable series resistor holding the output voltage constant. The value of this series resistance is varied by the control circuit in response to variations in current load and rectifier input voltage.

7. A shunt regulator varies the load resistance of the rectifier. The output voltage varies because of the increased or decreased load current drawn. The shunt regulator causes an additional variation in load current which in turn causes a voltage drop which compensates for variation in the output voltage due to loading by the circuits being powered.

8. Pulse-regulated power supplies have much lower power losses than series or parallel regulators.

9. Short bursts or pulses of power are applied to an LC filter which yields the DC component of the pulses. The width of these bursts determines the magnitude of the DC voltage. Variations in output voltage cause the width of these pulses to vary in a manner which reduces the output variation.

206

10. These variations cause the emitter voltage, and hence the input resistance, to vary.

11. Collector resistance is added so that variations in load current at the emitter do not greatly affect the collector current. As a result, the collector current maintains a fairly constant emitter voltage in spite of load current variations. That is, decreases in emitter voltage cause greater base and collector currents. Increases in emitter voltage cause reduced base and collector currents. In either case, the variations in emitter voltage caused by loading are offset by the changes in collector current.

12. The output of one stage is directly connected to the next.

Chapter 3

1. (a) Control of industrial processes. (b) Equipment simulation. (c) Navigational guidance. (d) Solving equations. (e) Position guns and radar antennas. (f) Provide data displays. (g) Medical electronics. (h) Processing of telemetering data. (i) Guiding of machine tools.

2. (a) It must provide very stable low gain. (b) It must draw a very small input current. (c) It must faithfully reproduce the input waveform.

3. A feedback amplifier.

4. $A_r = -\dfrac{R_t}{R_1}$

5. $e_o = -e_1 \left(\dfrac{R_t}{R_1}\right) - e_2 \left(\dfrac{R_t}{R_2}\right)$

Chapter 4

1. (a) Power supply variations, (b) changes in gain due to temperature variations, (c) changes in quiescent current due to temperature variations, (d) thermal noise voltages, and (e) changes in transistor base-to-emitter voltage as a result of temperature variations.

2. The difference amplifier.

3. The negative feedback voltage cancels a portion of the input voltage. The higher-frequency components of the input voltage are attenuated by the amplifier, and as a result, *less* feedback voltage at these frequencies is available.

4. (a) The gain with feedback times the maximum input voltage should not exceed the maximum output voltage, (b) the exter-

nal input resistor must be small in relation to the amplifier input resistance, (c) the input resistance (with external resistors) of the following stage must not be less than the maximum allowable load resistance.

5. The parallel combination of the collector load resistance and the input resistance of the next stage.

6. By adding base or emitter resistance. However, if unbypassed, emitter resistance will cause negative feedback.

7. Load resistance, common-base current gain, base resistance, and emitter resistance.

8. By solving the loop equations of the equivalent circuit.

9. By finding the circuit quantities which correspond to the input voltage divided by the input current.

10. By finding the circuit quantities which correspond to the output voltage divided by the output current.

Chapter 5

1. (a) Driving indicating devices, (b) driving conveyor belts at variable speeds, (c) positioning of automated machine tools, (d) operating valves, (e) rotating radar antennas, (f) positioning missile-guidence devices, (g) aiming large guns, and (h) providing remote control for mechanical controls.

2. The amplitude of the applied voltage and current.

3. The interaction between two separate windings energized by voltages which are 90 degrees out of phase with each other.

4. (a) The preamplifier, (b) driver, and (c) output stage.

5. It provides signal-voltage amplification.

6. It provides both amplification and two signals 180 degrees out of phase with respect to each other (paraphase).

7. It provides power amplification.

8. By negative feedback.

9. By using a centertapped output transformer.

10. To prevent self oscillation at the high end of the band of frequencies contained in the modulated carrier.

Chapter 6

1. (a) The AND function, (b) the OR function, (c) inversion, and (d) temporary data storage.

2. A pulse–no-pulse or two different voltage levels.

3. Yes–no, true–false, binary *1*–binary *0*, on–off, present–absent, or logical *1*–logical *0*.

4. It provides a logical-*1* output when *all* inputs are logical *1*.

5. It provides a logical-*1* output when *any* input is logical *1*.

6. It reverses the condition of the applied input signal.

7. It works like a pulse-operated toggle switch—has two stable states (two positions).

8. They are continuously generated pulses used to time digital-computer operations.

9. When base current is not present, the emitter-to-collector resistance is very high (open switch). When high base current flows, the emitter-to-collector resistance is very low (closed switch).

10. Delay time, rise time, storage time, and fall time.

Chapter 7

1. a. Signal inputs or specific conditions.
   b. Signal A *and* signal B must be logical *1* before the circuit output will be logical *1*.
   c. A or B must be logical *1*.
   d. Not A *or* B must be logical *1*.
   e. A *and* not B must be logical *1*.

2. This logic system consists of one basic circuit using only resistors and transistors. This circuit, (NOR circuit), can perform the AND and the OR functions.

3. This logic system uses RTL circuits with switching capacitors added.

4. Transistors are used as series and parallel switches to perform the AND and the OR functions.

5. Diodes are used as voltage-sensitive switches to couple logical signals from input to output when the AND and OR conditions are satisfied.

6. Low voltages are used to draw base currents directly from transistor bases. Diodes are used to perform the logic operations and to provide the small voltage variations.

7. It is an unsaturated direct-coupled logic.

8. A and $\overline{A}$ are inverted versions of each other.

9. Because $\overline{\overline{A} + \overline{B}}$ is equivalent to AB.

10. The NOR circuit.

1. A device which can assume one of two stable states. It is an electronically-activated toggle switch.

2. The cross-coupling between the collector and the base of the opposite transistor.

3. It can be considered as consisting of two cross-connected inverters. When one is operated, the other is driven to cutoff.

4. To bypass the coupling resistors used to cross-couple the inverter stages. As a result, switching time is decreased.

5. To ensure that the input trigger is applied only to the "off" transistor and does not saturate the "on" transistor.

6. Diodes are used to clamp the input-voltage swing between limits that will prevent saturation.

7. Register logic exists when a group of flip-flops are used to provide a group of bits.

Chapter 9

1. (a) The pulses to be counted are applied to the complementing input of a flip-flop.
   (b) The first pulse sets the flip-flop thus indicating a count of binary one.
   (c) The second pulse resets the flip-flop, the output of which is used to complement a second flip-flop. As a result, the second pulse also sets the second flip-flop and thus indicates a count of two.
   (d) The third pulse sets the first flip-flop but does not affect the second. The count is then the one stored in the first flip-flop and the two stored in the second. This represents a count of three, and so on.

2. The switching of the preceding flip-flop must occur before the next flip-flop is operated. When many flip-flops are used, there is a long delay from the time that the input pulse is applied to the time that it causes the highest-count flip-flop to be operated.

3. The logical-1 output of each flip-flop in the counter is ANDed with the pulses used to operate the lowest-order flip-flop. As a result, the same input pulse which operates the first stage simultaneously operates all stages that are normally operated. This arrangement is called "parallel counting."

4. The set or "F" output of the flip-flop has a gate voltage applied to it when the first complementing input gate sets the flip-flop. The output gate voltage is removed when the *second* complement input gate voltage is applied and resets the flip-flop. This second pulse returns the flip-flop to its original state. The flip-flop pro-

vides one gate voltage for every two input gate voltages, thus dividing by two. A string of many flip-flops in series will divide by 2, 4, 8, 16, 32, and so on.

5. To shape sine waves into square waves.

6. It is a circuit which possesses one normal state. However, when the input voltage reaches a pre-determined value, the circuit switches to a second state. The circuit remains in this second state until the input voltage returns to the switching value. Either transistor of the Schmitt trigger can be used to provide a gate voltage when the transistors switch their states.

7. It consists of a group of series-connected flip-flops, which in turn are connected in such a manner that the last one is coupled to the first. The "F" output of each flip-flop drives the set input of the next stage. Each time a flip-flop is reset, the trailing edge of the "F" output sets the next flip-flop. A timing pulse is periodically applied to all of the reset inputs. As a result, when one flip-flop is set, each successive timing pulse causes the next flip-flop in the ring to be set and the previously set flip-flop to be reset. When the last flip-flop is reset, the first one is set for a second time, thus closing the ring. The "F" outputs of each flip-flop are used to supply gate voltages. However, each gate voltage appears only once during the ring count.

Chapter 10

1. It is the condition whereby increasing the voltage applied to a device causes a decreased current flow, or decreasing the applied voltage causes an increasing current flow.

2. It is biased to operate in its normal resistance region. Trigger pulses then bring the device into the negative resistance region after which positive feedback drives it to a second stable operating point. The device is reset when a second pulse brings it from the second operating point back to the first.

3. They are negative-resistance devices capable of operating in millimicroseconds (nanoseconds).

4. The voltage used to trigger the tunnel diode is provided by more than one input source. As a result, AND and OR functions can be realized.

5. The Goto pair consists of two tunnel diodes connected in series and energized by a common voltage source. They are biased so that when one conducts the remaining voltage is not sufficient to allow the second to conduct. As a result, the diode which does conduct indicates one of two stable states.

6. (a) The temperature dependance of their characteristics and (b) the interaction between stages.

7. By pulse powering each stage and by a phase-locked system of triggering.

8. When groups of circuits are operated at fixed times which are not the same for all circuits.

Chapter 11

1. They are used to switch the currents to the cores.

2. The flux direction within the core remains in one of two directions and thus stores a logical *1* or a logical *0*. Read-in and read-out is accomplished by applying current pulses to read-in and read-out coils.

3. The OR function is performed when any *one* of a few input coils can be energized to set the core. The AND function is performed when *all* input coils must be simultaneously energized in order to set the core.

4. These are used because the same module can. be connected in many different ways in order to perform many different computer functions.

5. The blocking oscillator.

Chapter 12

1. So that production lines can be set up to manufacture large quantities of a few simple circuits. These simple circuits, on the small printed-circuit boards, are then placed in a common frame and interconnected in order to perform more complex operations.

2. The circuits of a computer must be capable of rapid replacement so that proper computer operation can be quickly restored when malfunctions are detected. The removable modules of modular construction make this possible.

3. Flat-board, cylindrical, and square block.

4. Plastic and epoxy embeddment.

5. Layers of vaporized metals, semiconductors, and insulators are deposited on a glass base. These layers form the circuit.

Chapter 13

1. Groups of signal generators and circuits used to operate modules in a manner which simulates actual computer operation.

2. To localize malfunctions in modules which have been removed from computers during maintenance.

3. The characteristics of a transistor are plotted on the face of an oscilloscope. The collector voltages and base currents are varied in steps, each step causing one of the curves to appear on the scope. After all the steps are applied to the transistor, the complete family of curves appears on the face of the scope.

4. The circuit power-supply voltages are increased or decreased about 10 percent from the rated values. At this point, circuits which are on the verge of failure will breakdown. Thus, these circuits fail during test and not during actual operation. Circuits which are sound will not fail under these conditions. As a result, fewer circuits malfunction during actual operation and the computer is more reliable.

5. A means of causing each operation of a computer to be performed in order to detect any fault that might occur and permit locating and identifying the malfunctioning circuits.

Index

Flip-flop
circuits, 127-139
counting, 127-139
definition of, 74
explanation of, 113-125
logic, 123-125
nonsaturating, 121-123
saturating, 116-121
Forward voltage-drop test, 197
Frequency division, 75, 76, 131-133
counting, 131-133
Functions, logic, 73, 74

G

Gain
equation
current, 55
voltage, 52, 54, 55
test, saturation, 194
Gated bridge-rectifier, 26-28
Goto-pair
majority-control inputs, 152-155
phased clock pulses, 154, 155
phase-locked operation, 153-155
tunnel-diode logic, 151-155

H

High-gain operational amplifier, 46-49
Human notation counting, 141

I

Input resistance equation, 51, 54, 57
Inversion function, 96
Inverted-OR function, 96, 97, 98
Inverted circuit, definition of, 74

J

Junction leakage test, 195

L

Leakage test, junction, 195
Logic
AC, 98
circuits, 87-112
(CML), 92-95
(DCTL), 89, 94, 95
(DL), 91, 92, 94, 95
dynamic, 98, 99
flip-flop, 123-125
function, 73, 74
(LLL), 92, 94, 95
(RCTL), 89, 94, 95
register, 124, 125
(RTL), 87-89, 94, 95
static, 98, 99
system, 87
Logical indicators, 137
Loop
B-H, tester, 197, 198
-current equation, 54
-voltage equation, 54
Lowest-order counting, 127
Low-Level Logic (LLL), 92, 94, 95

M

Machine notation counting, 141
Magnetic cores
characteristics of, 157, 158
computer systems, 161, 162
logic operations, 161
reset drive coil, 159, 160
transistor driven, 157-162
Majority-control inputs, Goto-pair, 152-155
Marginal checking, 200, 201
Mechanization and automation, 174-175
Microminiaturization, 179-188
Miniaturization, 179-188
Minority-carrier storage test, 196

217

219

COMPUTER BASICS SERIES

Table of Contents

For Other Volumes

VOL. IV—Digital Computers—Storage and Logic Circuitry

VOL. V—Analog and Digital Computers—Organization, Programming, and Maintenance

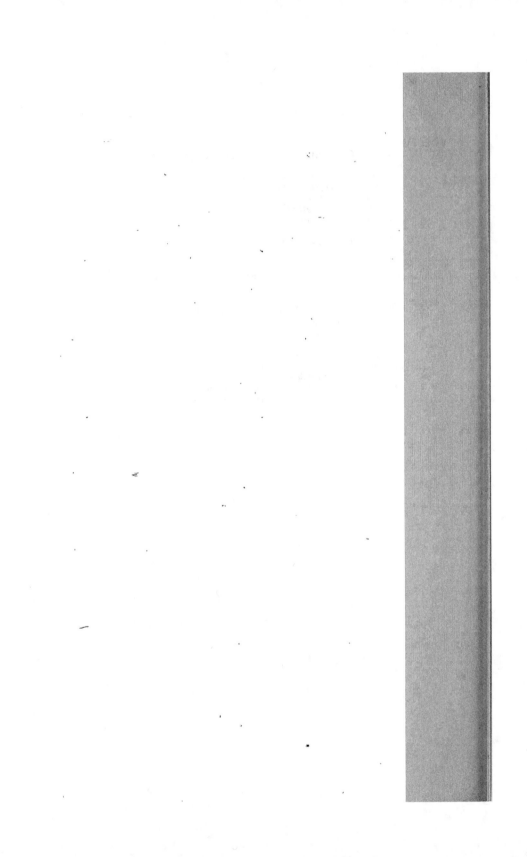

www.ingramcontent.com/pod-product-compliance
Lightning Source LLC
LaVergne TN
LVHW012203040326
832903LV00003B/93